PATRICK McNEIL, creator of designmeltdown.com

THE WEB DESIGNER'S volume 4
IDEA BOOK

inspiration from today's best web design trends, themes and styles

HOW
BOOKS
Cincinnati, Ohio
www.howdesign.com

The Mobile Web Designer's Idea Book, Volume 4. Copyright © 2014 by Patrick McNeil. Manufactured in the United States of America. All rights reserved. No other part of this book may be reproduced in any form or by any electronic or mechanical means including information storage and retrieval systems without permission in writing from the publisher, except by a reviewer, who may quote brief passages in a review. Published by HOW Books, an imprint of F+W Media, Inc., 10151 Carver Road, Suite 200, Blue Ash, Ohio 45242. (800) 289-0963. First edition.

For more excellent books and resources for designers, visit www.howdesign.com.

17 16 15 14   5 4 3 2 1

ISBN-13: 978-1-4403-3315-6

Distributed in Canada by Fraser Direct
100 Armstrong Avenue
Georgetown, Ontario, Canada L7G 5S4
Tel: (905) 877-4411

Distributed in the U.K. and Europe by F&W Media International, LTD
Brunel House, Forde Close, Newton Abbot, TQ12 4PU, UK
Tel: (+44) 1626 323200, Fax: (+44) 1626 323319
Email: enquiries@fwmedia.com

Distributed in Australia by Capricorn Link
P.O. Box 704, Windsor, NSW 2756 Australia
Tel: (02) 4560-1600

Edited by Scott Francis
Designed by Claudean Wheeler
Production coordinated by Greg Nock

a content + ecommerce company

Dedication

For Angela, my biggest builder.

About the Author

To say that Patrick McNeil is obsessed with web design is a bit of an understatement. What began as a simple exploration of design on his blog, www.designmeltdown.com, eventually turned into a bestselling series of books. With a passion for technology and design, Patrick has found himself at home on the web—where these two areas merge. His love of design drives him to obsess over the trends and patterns you see collected in this book. Beyond observing trends, Patrick is focused on front-end development techniques, user-centered design practices and teaching designers to effectively leverage the web as a design medium. Patrick teaches in the graphic design department at the University of Missouri in St. Louis where he focuses on the interactive design component of the program. For more information about Patrick, visit his personal site, www.pmcneil.com, or follow him on Twitter @designmeltdown.

Word From the Author

I always save this little section for the very end, as the very last thing I write in my books. I do this because it is easy to sum up a book right as you finish it. It is bittersweet. Obviously, it is fun and exciting to finish something big, but at the same time, it means I have to go do other stuff. And frankly, writing these books is about as much fun I can imagine having while doing something that can be called "work."

What I love about the web more than anything is that it is always changing. Year to year things are never the same: new technologies, new tools, new trends, new styles, new designers and so on. Through the process of creating these books I get to dig into all of that, look at thousands of websites and ultimately pick out all the gems I love. Can you imagine a better gig? I sure can't.

I am really excited to introduce a new feature that comes with this book. As you may or may not know, I have written three previous volumes—plus a mobile idea book. There are a handful of topics that I have touched on in pretty much every volume, and other themes that are related to material appearing across the books, though not the same exact topic. For example, retro themed designs have taken on several forms over the years and have appeared in different ways in several of my books. Because of this I have created a cross reference tool which you can find at the link below. This will point you to chapters in my other books that you might find relevant given the topic you're looking at.

Thank you again for picking up this latest volume, and I sincerely hope it gives you the inspiration you seek.

Cross Reference

Many of the design patterns referenced in this book can also be found in other volumes from this series. Even better, many of the topics are interrelated and are great to view in combination. With this in mind I have put together a free, printable index available on www.thewebdesignersideabook.com/index. Just look up the topic your viewing and it will point you to related material across all of my books. As I publish new books I will continue to update this free resource.

Future Books

If you would like to submit your designs for possible use in future books, please visit www.thewebdesignersideabook.com to sign up for my mailing list. You will be informed of book releases, calls for entries and other information directly related to the books.

QR CODES

Throughout this book you will find QR codes. Each chapter will have one at the beginning. If you scan these codes, they will take you to landing pages where you can find links to all of the samples presented in the given chapter. This means you can scan the code and quickly launch and try out the sites I have selected without having to type the URL into your device.

In time, many of these sites will change, and some will disappear all together, but this is the nature of the web and my books are but a snapshot in time. However, I do believe the majority will remain the same and accessible. Eventually I may update the landing pages with full size images as presented in the book. This way, sometime long in the future the QR codes will still serve a useful purpose.

For those of you that have no idea what a QR code is, it is essentially a special type of barcode. You can install a QR code scanner on your smartphone or tablet that will allow you to scan the tag and it will take you to a URL. This prevents you from having to key the URL into your phone. It is actually a really handy way to get a URL loaded onto a phone or tablet. Note that many bar code scanner apps also scan QR codes. In fact, my favorite bar code scanner on my Android device scans QR codes as well: the app is creatively titled Barcode Scanner.

As you read this book, keep your smartphone handy. If you see a design you like, you can simply scan the code and browse the live site. This is particularly handy given the ever-increasing importance of mobile and how annoying it is to try to key a URL into a phone.

PORTFOLIO SITES

As with each previous volume of my Idea Books, I like to focus the first portion of the book on a secondary topic. Volume 1 featured colors, Volume 2 featured the basic elements of design, and Volume 3 featured various technologies that impact web design. This new volume focuses on taking an in-depth look at online portfolio sites.

It may not be all that surprising, but the most common types of sites people submit for my books are agency and portfolio sites. This is also an area that I am asked about very frequently. With this in mind, I am excited to analyze trends and patterns more extensively in this specific area.

Even if you don't need to design a portfolio site, I believe you will find the categories very interesting. Many of the topics I have collected for this section are entirely new to me and represent some interesting ways to look at design patterns. For example, I am particularly intrigued by the regional chapter that shows the differences in portfolios from around the world.

While I completely understand that we think of an individual person when we think of a portfolio, I am also including agencies in this section. Though most of the sites presented here are for a single person, there are some collections here dedicated to agencies of different types. You will also see some agency sites peppered throughout the other sections.

Finally, I want to point out that the sites collected here are not limited to those in the design world. I have attempted to collect a wide range of sites that fall into many areas that require an online portfolio. These include portfolios for designers, photographers, painters and even sports figures.

01/

PORTFOLIO STYLES AND TRENDS

At the heart of my Idea Books are design styles and trends. With this in mind I want to lead off this section on these topics. You will perhaps recognize many of these approaches from my previous books. The difference here, of course, is that they are 100% portfolio sites. At first I thought it would be hard to build out this section, but once I got going it was actually really hard to stop. I could fill volumes of books with categories of styles in just the portfolio genre.

I think there is real value in looking at a specific niche of web design in such a detailed way. It is amazing to see just how many patterns emerge. As a result, we can focus on the common ways in which people solve various problems. In the end you will hopefully find some fresh ideas to inspire your portfolio designs and any other type of work as well.

01/Super Clean

The Super Clean chapter is one I include in all of my Idea Books. As I have said in the past, this style embodies all of my favorite qualities and the sites here are typically the ones I admire the most. Sites that fit in here must display the cleanest and most beautiful designs. And most often they contain a clean, spacious layout that is easy to consume. Let's dissect a few examples to see what I mean.

A perfect example is the MING Labs website **(FIGURE 1)**. This site embraces a minimalist approach and is void of any structural design elements. This allows the designer to focus the user's attention through a clear (and beautiful) typographic hierarchy. Though the site might appear simple, its detailed nuances are gorgeous and leave nothing undone. Notice how clean the design feels. It is full of space and one can easily digest its content—a perfect example of the super clean style at work.

Another example that easily fits into this category—and is equally easy to love—is the Heikopaiko site **(FIGURE 2)**. Again the site leans toward the minimalist mindset, as most Super Clean sites do. But here, it feels less sparse, and yet it still has a clarity to it that is very welcome. Notice how you have no trouble scanning the site and consuming its content. There is no confusion in the flow of the document, no mixed messages, and no details left unattended. Super Clean sites like this one are so refined that it is almost annoying; annoying because it shows just how perfect a website can be. Frankly, this site feels so spot on that you feel like you're looking at a Photoshop comp and not a live website.

Finally, let's look at the portfolio site of Aaron Smith **(FIGURE 3)**. Again we find that the site is full of space and relies on a really strong typographic hierarchy. Another pattern starts to emerge, though. Many of the sites I consider Super Clean make use of a single stream of content: rather than having sidebar elements and extra things that confuse the layout, they rely on a single column. This reinforces the content hierarchy and is a powerful component of making something feel clean. It seems that this would also be a great way to make a site easy to translate into a mobile structure. Perhaps some of these sites even took a mobile-first approach, which would explain the pattern.

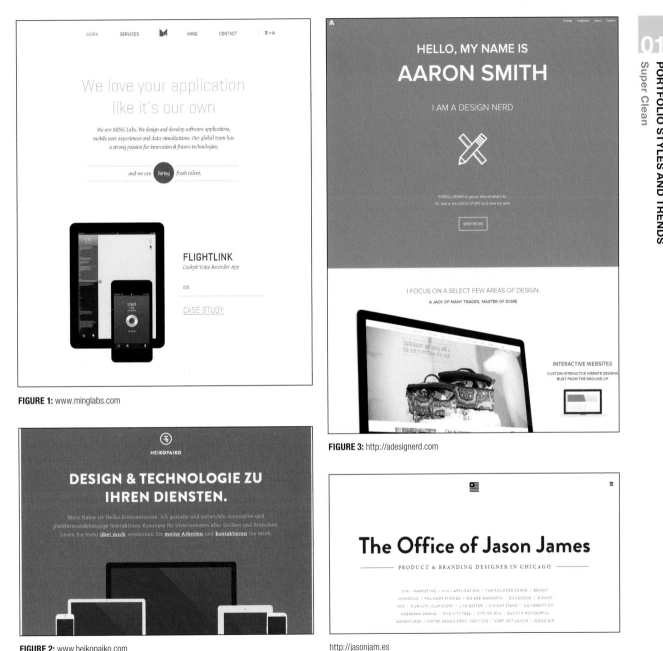

FIGURE 1: www.minglabs.com

FIGURE 2: www.heikopaiko.com

FIGURE 3: http://adesignerd.com

http://jasonjam.es

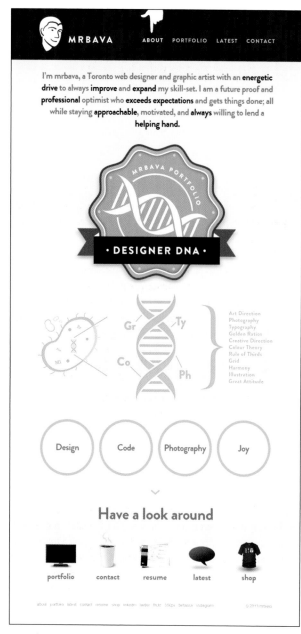

www.mrbava.com

http://robdavisdesigner.co.uk

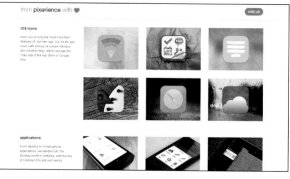

www.pixerience.com

http://lukaslinden.net

01/Illustrated Designs

I have long been an advocate of illustration in design if only for a single reason: It almost always leads to a really unique design. Want to blend in with the herd? Rely on stock photos or artwork that anyone can use (and everyone does). Want to completely stand out? Make original artwork a component of your design. No one will have your exact style combined with your ideas. It is a great way to make your work pop. Granted, we aren't all great illustrators, but I believe that we can all create something from scratch.

Another huge potential perk to this style is the current popularity of what is known as the Flat Design style (see page 080 in this book). A flat design is void of depth and decoration and is very minimalist. By working in some unique illustrated elements our work can really pop. So, again, illustrations can really make your work stand out, and given the current style that is so popular, it can stand out *even* more.

Symphony Online **(FIGURE 1)** is a lovely example of this. It uses beautiful type, subtle textures, solid colors and decorated edge treatments (all of those topics, by the way, are covered in *The Web Designer's Idea Book, Volume 3*). All of these elements are very popular and in style. The site genuinely feels relevant in the current design world. But notice how the illustration adds uniqueness to the design that makes it stand on its own. The site doesn't at all feel like yet another "me too!" design. In my humble opinion, the illustrations are what make this site really pop.

Next I want to look at the portfolio site of William Cole **(FIGURE 2)**. In this case, I would say that the site doesn't fit into the current style at all. In fact, the fundamental design of the site goes right against everything that is trendy and popular right now. In some ways this works against the site—or at least creates an uphill battle for the site's designer. If you break with convention, and even go opposite of convention, you have to really bring your A game. In this case, I think the designer successfully did just that. Yes, the site isn't trendy, but it feels extremely unique. Even more, it seems that the site's style reflects that of the artist behind it. It has more character, and you get the sense that an artist made it. Look through his work and I think you will agree that this resonates perfectly with his body of work and personal style.

FIGURE 1: www.symphonyonline.co.uk

FIGURE 2: www.perpetuo.it

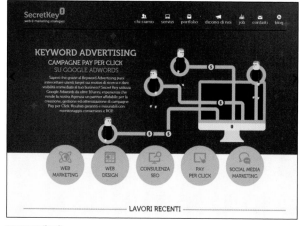

www.secretkey.it

http://enniscreates.com

www.thesearethings.com

www.creativemints.com

www.ipolecat.com

www.socialforces.com

01/Masonry Styles

This style is named for a jQuery plug-in that is largely responsible for the results you see here. The Masonry plug-in[1] organizes rectangular items that vary in size and dimension by laying them out in such a way that they all fit together perfectly. It rearranges them like stones in a wall and the result is a solid structure of images or other content. Though this is not a new thing, it is incredibly prominent in the world of portfolio design. As such, I thought it was appropriate to highlight the approach here. Another popular plug-in that does pretty much the same thing but with a few other options is Isotope[2].

The portfolio of Alexa Falcone **(FIGURE 1)** is a perfect example of this. On this site you can clearly see the collage of images with a variety of sizes and dimensions. If you open the site and resize your browser, you will quickly notice that the elements rearrange to fill the available space. Using the Masonry plug-in, the content perfectly fills up any screen size and best of all, the plug-in does all the hard work for you.

Another great example is Glauce Cerveira's **(FIGURE 2)** portfolio site. Here you also see a grid of images neatly arranged into a solid wall of content. In this case, you will also see that the "bricks" being arranged in this way can include any type of content—you are not limited to images alone. Instead you can have a series of containers that get positioned magically, whether they contain images, text or articles.

If you are considering this approach, there is perhaps a single gotcha you may encounter. Since the plug-in is arranging the elements in the grid system, you have little control over what goes where. You can sort of place things generally based on the order you put them into the page. But as the screen size changes it will move things around. So, if the exact order or placement of the elements is critical to you, this may be a problem.

Finally, I want to mention a simpler alternative. If you are going to use this style and you find that all of your items have the same width (height can vary), you need not use a plug-in to get the same results. Simply look into using CSS-based text columns with the column-count CSS property[3]. This turns a block of content (including images) in a container into multiple columns inside of the same container. The results look the same as the Masonry style (when the items are equal width), but without the complications of using a jQuery plug-in.

[1] The Masonry plug-in: http://masonry.desandro.com
[2] The Isotope plug-in: http://isotope.metafizzy.co
[3] A great article on CSS based content columns: http://css-tricks.com/snippets/css/multiple-columns

FIGURE 1: www.alexafalcone.com

FIGURE 2: www.glauce.com

www.poddapontiarchitetti.it

http://jamesnash.net

www.danielmillroy.com

www.indubitablee.com

www.balinov.com

www.vbg.si/en

01/One Page Folios

The one page folio is certainly not a new phenomenon, and yet it is rather easy to find examples of one page portfolio sites with styles and trends all their own. In fact, there are so many approaches to the one page folio that I was tempted to do multiple chapters on the topic, each highlighting a different subsection. Rather than go overboard, let's instead dissect a few common examples from this carefully selected collection.

Cody Eason's one page site **(FIGURE 1)** demonstrates many trends at once—which is really remarkable given the rather sparse design. For starters, he begins his site with an extremely short introduction. When we think about recruiters looking at potential job candidates, it is not hard to imagine how welcome such a statement is. There is power in knowing your core identity—especially in an industry with such closely related and diverse roles to fill. It is tempting to draw back and not want to pigeonhole yourself. Tempting though it may be, I can't express how much I appreciate concise and specific statements. Short of showing your best work, I think this is perhaps one of the most important elements you can put into your portfolio site. And with a one-pager like this, you guarantee that everyone hitting your site will see this intro and know what you are all about.

Second, Cody's site makes use of somewhat unusual navigation. It isn't the typical list of links across the top. Instead, we find that the links are listed along the side. This is actually a pattern that we are finding on many sites and it works really well, especially for in-page navigation such as this.

Finally, the site embraces the flat design model, resulting in a prime example of yet another current trend. The site lacks depth and decorative elements (or ornate containers for content) for the structure. This is not an insult but rather a compliment. Designers can be really tempted into making monstrosities of portfolio sites, packed with all the things they wish they could do for clients. In contrast, Cody's portfolio is super clean and to the point. His work is showcased beautifully and the site portrays him well. Frankly, it is amazing how effective such a simple approach can be. And perhaps that is the rub: "Simple" isn't always so easy to come by; and instead it requires a great deal of effort.

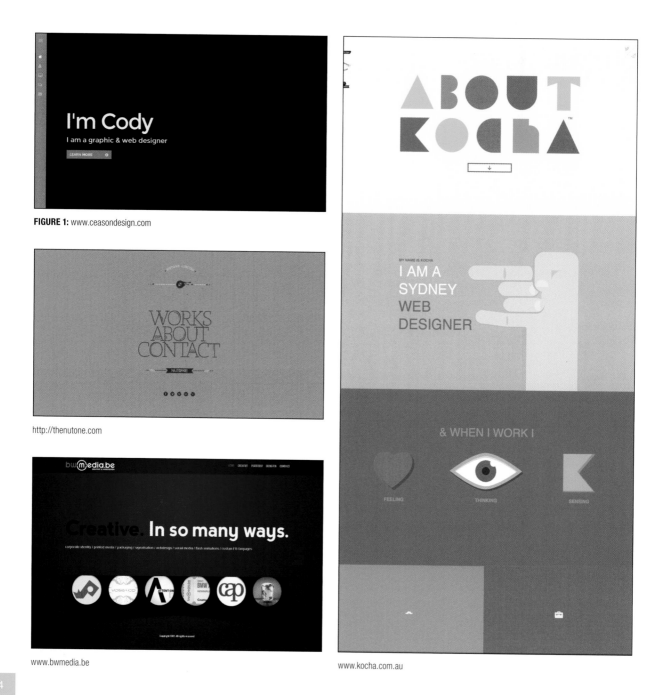

FIGURE 1: www.ceasondesign.com

http://thenutone.com

www.bwmedia.be

www.kocha.com.au

www.colincoolidge.com/worksamples

www.davegarwacke.com

www.socketstudios.com

www.kokodigital.co.uk

01/Front and Center

For this chapter, I want to highlight portfolio sites that don't hide the portfolio pieces away on sub pages; instead they push them to the front page. But these sites don't stop there—they make the work the primary focus of the home page by placing images front and center. Most often this is done through placement on the page and usually with very large images. As a result, the work becomes the primary focus. If your work is amazing this is a great way to structure your site. Rather than mess around with sales pitches or fancy introductions you just get to the point. In many cases the work is so outstanding that you hardly need to say anything else. It is the hook that draws people in and makes them really want to work with the individual or agency that did the work.

My favorite example here is the Hidden Depth website **(FIGURE 1)**. This agency website is an extremely minimalist design that is essentially void of any decoration. As you can see in the screenshot, a large sample portfolio piece is placed near the top of the home page. This single portfolio piece serves as a gateway to the portfolio as a whole, which is packed with diverse and beautiful work. (It always helps when you have a great body of work to back things up.) Another interesting aspect of the large and prominent portfolio piece is the way the site handles as the screen changes size. On large screens, it is a collection of devices and computers. As the screen shrinks, it becomes a single laptop image with a website on it. Finally, as it condenses down to the mobile version, it showcases a trio of iPhones with mobile websites. It is a small detail, but I think it is ingenious how they have tailored the space to fit the medium.

Another common approach in this section is to provide a very large grid of work with almost no supportive content or elements. Sarah Coulton's portfolio **(FIGURE 2)** is a prime example of this approach. This bare bones site gives the viewer almost nothing beyond the portfolio pieces. Again, if you have really great work, this is a great way to simply let the art speak for you. In this case, we get a glimpse into Sarah's work and her overall style. The one risk here is that there is not a lot of information, so be darn sure your work is saying what you need it to! It is also important to give people a way to reach you. Don't get so carried away with being minimalist that you leave out your contact info.

FIGURE 1: http://hiddendepth.ie

FIGURE 2: http://sarahcoulton.com

http://milee.co/works.html

www.orcunkilic.com/works

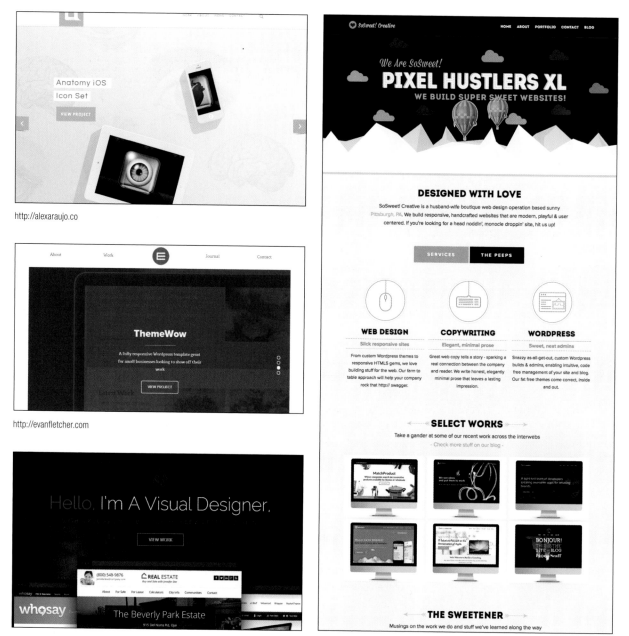

http://alexaraujo.co

http://evanfletcher.com

http://zindustry.com

http://sosweetcreative.com

01/Atypical Portfolios

In each of my books I feature a section on atypical sites. For this volume, I decided to dedicate the chapter to atypical portfolio sites. However, portfolio sites as a whole are pretty much atypical. Though we find common patterns, there is such an extreme range of approaches that the sites here don't feel too much off-the-beaten-path. That said, each of these sites is unique and puts a rather distinct spin on the portfolio.

A lovely example of this is the agency site for Creanet **(FIGURE 1)**. In general, most websites lean toward a vertical orientation. That is, they tend to be tall with content stacked on top of itself. From time to time we find a horizontal scrolling site (something that has fallen out of style for the most part). This site is not a horizontal scroller, yet it is horizontally oriented. This is why I placed it into this particular category: It just felt atypical and distinct. The animations on the home page also make this site worth a visit. Though the design is extremely restrained, it is a joy to browse.

The basic building blocks of the web are rectangular in shape, which makes the organic and unusual shapes found on AltSpace **(FIGURE 2)** all the more interesting and atypical. What I find even more amazing is that these unusual shapes scale to fit the browser. Not only do they scale, they actually change shape so they fill the space (much like the Masonry-based sites found on page 010). The developer has accomplished this using Scalable Vector Graphics (SVG)—the web's version of vector graphics. I am intrigued with how the site balances showcasing an incredible body of work and a unique interface that shows off their coding skills. This is a lethal combo that is remarkably effective.

While I do not advocate doing something atypical simply for the sake of being different, I do advocate for thinking creatively, pushing boundaries and generally testing the limits of the web—especially when this can be done in concert with beautiful design. It is hard to argue with an extremely functional site that demonstrates progressive, forward-thinking results.

In my opinion, the best way to arrive at atypical results is to simply focus on the needs of the content. Carefully consider the content and how the audience will engage with it to discover the details of the individual (or company) behind the site. From there, form a solution without regard to the many assumed norms that constrain us. In theory, the results will be unique (and perhaps even atypical), but will retain an extremely functional core, which is far more important than being different.

FIGURE 1: www.creanet.es

FIGURE 2: http://altspace.com

http://progetty.it

http://www.ideator.si

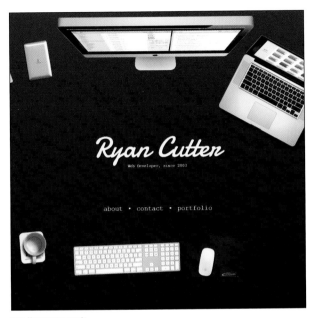

http://ryancutter.co.uk

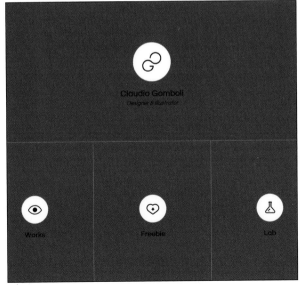

http://pgrdesign.net

http://marisapassos.com

http://theeggs.biz

01/Thematic Portfolios

As you will find in several places throughout this book, the modern design aesthetic based on flat designs leaves a lot of room for anything contrasting to stand out. Thematic design is one design approach that leaves a lasting impression and can help one stand out from the crowd.

As much as I love a super clean and minimalist approach to design it can be such a relief to see something new and different. A pattern I've noticed is that the individuals with "fancy" portfolios typically have weaker work, and those with crazy simple ones have the best work. So it might seem that going a bit over the top with a thematic portfolio is a mistake. It's not, though. I think it makes good sense to leverage your creative skills to make a portfolio site that stands out.

Case in point, take a look at the portfolio site for Robby Leonardi **(FIGURE 1)**. He turned his site into a fully interactive theme based on Super Mario Brothers. It is nothing short of incredible, and this site received a lot of fanfare. I recall noticing it showing up in email newsletters from many of the biggest names in web design (*Smashing Magazine*, Web-Designer Depot and more). The site certainly places the focus on the form of the portfolio and far less on the design work. But it is hard to argue with the amount of exposure the site received (and continues to receive). I guarantee if you produce yet another flat mini-malistic design based on solid colors and monochromatic photos with white text on the top—that you will *not* be getting such attention. Not that your site will suck, it just won't stand out and warrant this level of attention.

Another example that really stands out to me is Matthew Jordan's portfolio site **(FIGURE 2)**. His site is extremely thematic and seems to pretty much ignore just about every modern design trend imaginable. In a way, it feels a bit dated in that the style harkens back to what was rather popular about six years ago. And yet, it doesn't feel entirely trapped in that world. Somehow it transcends the style that was and applies the same approach in a modern way. For example, the site is a single page, it doesn't have a traditional header, and most importantly it doesn't have the decorative frame that would give it a fixed size. I applaud Matthew for using such a rich visual style that is not the norm. In the end, I think it is true to his personality and the style of work he produces. And isn't that the point of a portfolio in the first place, to share your own personal style, whatever that may be?

FIGURE 1: www.rleonardi.com/interactive-resume

http://elegantseagulls.com

FIGURE 2: www.matthewdjordan.com

http://speed-motion.com.ua

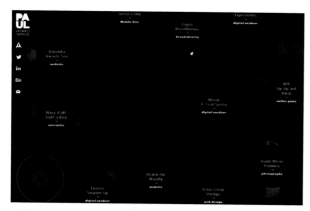

http://bornin82.com

www.designzillas.com

www.twistedstudio.com

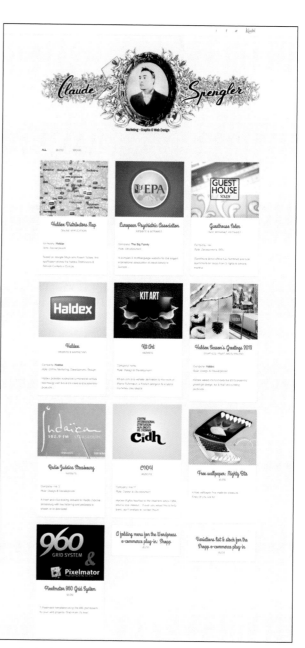

www.cla-ude.net

01/Landing Page Portfolios

For some designers a simple landing page is sufficient; for others it is a good starting point. Online landing pages are kind of like business cards but with a digital twist. Most often they point to various destinations, like social networks or portfolio services like Behance. Though these super simple landing pages are light on content, they can still provide a glimpse into the individual they represent.

For example, consider these two landing pages: Vlad Rodriguez **(FIGURE 1)** and Minnix **(FIGURE 2)**. Vlad is a painter, while Minnix is user experience (UX) designer and front-end developer. Certainly these two career fields contrast rather sharply, and I would say that the incredibly simple landing pages each of them has accurately reflects their respective types of work.

It's also really hard not to love Manuel Moreale's crazy simple landing page site **(FIGURE 3)**. As you can see in the screenshot he is a designer that fully embraces the minimalist mindset. If you visit the live site, you will see that the darker text after his e-mail address rotates through various statements. What a simple yet interesting way to create a unique experience—and perhaps even a memorable one for those visiting. Again, I am floored at how something so simple can convey so much. In some ways, it is a real demonstration of the power of design. The more I see how so little can perform so well I am reminded just how meaningful every last aspect of a design should be.

If you lack an online presence, I challenge you to start with a simple page such as this. You should be able to put it together in a very short amount of time. As a result, you will have a single place to refer people to for information all about you, even if it just directs users to Twitter and Behance. It is still beneficial and gives you a starting point for building your own online presence.

FIGURE 1: www.vladrodriguez.com

FIGURE 2: http://minnixio.com

hello@manuelmoreale.com: i love minimalism

FIGURE 3: http://manuelmoreale.com

www.janixpacle.com

www.andrewkapish.com

http://fuelthemes.net

http://tylersanguinette.com

http://ryansrich.com

01/Responsive Portfolios

Perhaps the biggest challenge designers and developers face right now is sorting through the madness we call responsive web design. Designing and creating a site that will work on any screen size is nothing short of an epic challenge. As such, I really wanted to show a lot of variety in this section. So collected here is the largest set of images you will find in this book. This is an area where inspiration can pay off in a big way. Dig through the samples here and discover how others have faced the very problems you will face when building an online portfolio.

In most cases, like the portfolio of Michael Sevilla **(FIGURE 1)**, the flow from large screen to small is natural and nearly obvious. The grid of images slowly condenses down to a single column and the navigation finds its way just below the logo. It feels natural and almost like it was meant to be. We find much the same results on the Applove site **(FIGURE 2)**. Here, bands of horizontal content naturally transition to a single stacked set of elements as the contents of each row slowly condense into a single column. This is the type of approach we find often, and it is an example of what I consider the single biggest structural pattern of modern web design.

Flash back about ten years ago, and the basic structure of the web was marked by clear headers for logos and navigation, sidebars for sub navigation, an obvious content region, and a footer to finish it off. Quite often, the design was unified by some sort of containing structure that framed everything in place. These containers unified all the elements and created pockets to place everything into. Jump back into the present, and we find that responsive design has pretty much sealed the fate of this approach. Those fancy containers and holders of content are a nightmare to style in a responsive world. Instead, we find that horizontal bands of content do this job wonderfully. Each band can adjust as needed and can continue to stack on top of each other. These bands of content are the modern day standard for how to structure content. Look through the samples in this chapter, and throughout the book, you will find it over and over again.

FIGURE 1: http://svla.co

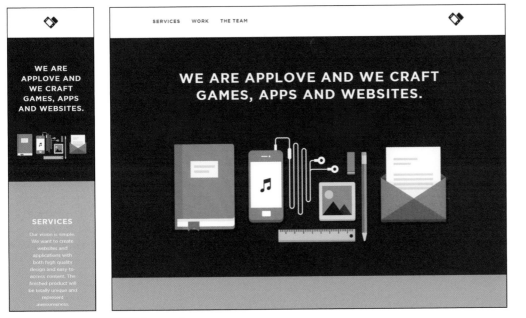

FIGURE 2: www.applove.se

http://janne.me

www.asylummarketing.com

http://doabackflip.com

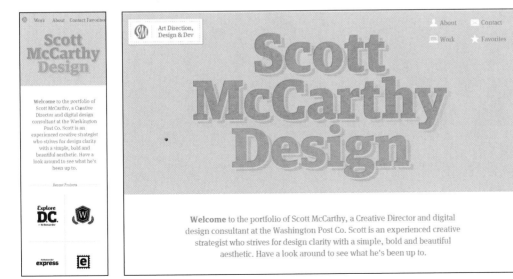

www.scottmccarthydesign.com

http://residence-mixte.com

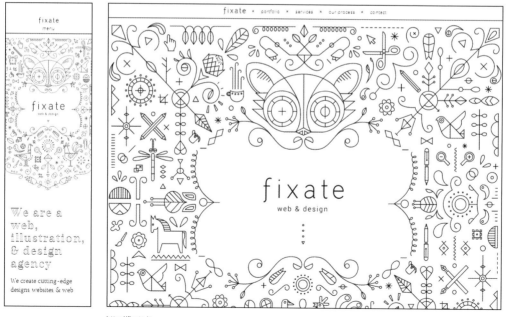

http://fixate.it

www.philippehong.com

www.antro.ca/en

02/

PORTFOLIOS BY REGION

In all my years of collecting websites and categorizing them I have never attempted to analyze styles or patterns based on geographic region. Naturally we find that there is a huge range of styles and ideas at work in locations around the world. Aesthetics and culture play a significant role in design, and this is revealed in the design of portfolio sites from various regions.

There is a dynamic to analyzing sites based on region that is perplexing. If my intention is to showcase beautiful web design, and I am looking at web designs based on regions, and each region of the world has its own definition of beauty—what aesthetic parameters do I base my selections on? A choice must be made, and so I choose focus on sites that are beautiful to me and the audience I speak to. This is a necessary distinction to point out.

To be honest, I expected to find a radical range of styles—each one vividly connected to a specific part of the world. It seems to me that ten years ago, the web was more divided, and it was easier to notice a difference based on region. But as you browse the sites collected here, on first look you will likely have no idea where in the world the sites originated from! I find it fascinating as you focus in on the details of these sites, you will notice small details that distinguish one from the other and give subtle hints as to the region of the world represented.

A fantastic example of this is the small set of sites from Asia. My expectation with this particular section was that they would somehow fit into a stereotype of the region. The funny thing is that I am not even sure what that means! Stereotypes are kind of like that, and as you dig into them you may find your expectations overturned.

The question this naturally leads to is puzzling: Are these simply agencies in the Asian region that are attempting to appeal to Western audiences? If so, then mission accomplished. Or do these sites fit into expectations within Asian culture, which has gravitated towards the same styles as the West?

02/European Union

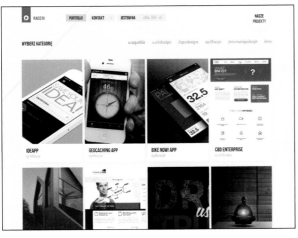

http://radziu.org

www.jenslehmann.com

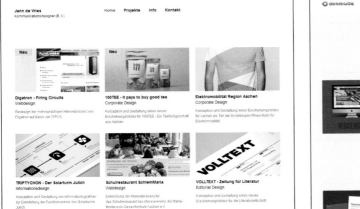

www.min-style.de

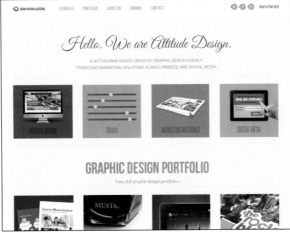

www.attitudedesign.co.uk

02/Eastern Europe

http://cheesebanana.com

http://porcupinecolors.com

www.pageinteractive.pl

www.sasahuzjak.com

02/North America

http://pauljohns.com

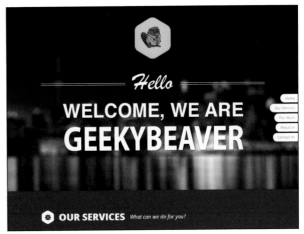

www.geekybeaver.ca

http://burciaga.co

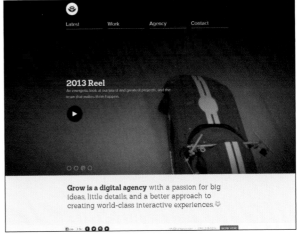

www.thisisgrow.com

02/South America

http://leozakour.com

www.publer.com.br

http://isabelarodrigues.org

http://igorodrigues.com.br

/Asia

www.cleancutcrew.com

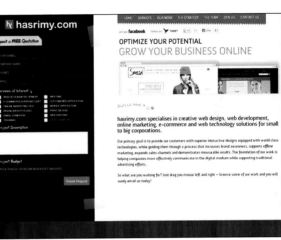

www.hasrimy.com

http://arunpattnaik.com

http://webcoursesagency.com

02/Oceana

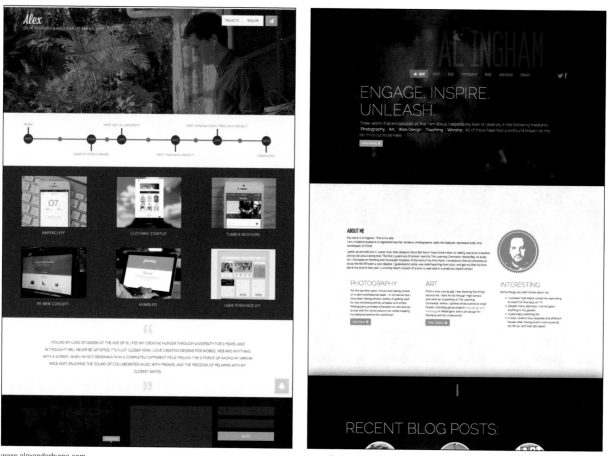

www.alexanderbyrne.com

www.alingham.com

02/Middle East

http://url.com.tr

http://simpleia.com

www.pixelwrapped.com

03 /

One Man Show • The Micro Agency (fewer than 10 people) • Medium Agencies (10 to 50 people) • Large Agencies (50 people or more)

PORTFOLIOS BY AGENCY SIZE

Much like the portfolio sites by region, I have never really assessed portfolio styles based on the size of the agency. In the following four sets I showcase portfolios of individuals, micro agencies (which I define as fewer than 10 people), medium agencies (10 to 50 people) and large agencies (with 50 or more people). In this case we can observe some clear differences.

It seems that as we go from the smallest to the largest of agency websites, the portfolios go from very stylized to much more generic. I think this is because individuals reflect their own individual styles and capabilities—and smaller agencies have fewer personalities to represent. A large agency has so many people and teams that it is likely they can take on many more types of work and produce a tremendous range of styles. As such, it just doesn't make as much sense to put on the facade of a single style so they tend to gravitate toward minimalist and very streamlined designs. Scan through the sample sets from small to large and you will no doubt notice this. At first I thought this was a coincidence based on the sites I happened to collect. But as I looked further it held true in most cases. What I found was that often times the smaller shops and individuals tried to look more stylistic, while the larger shops almost never tried to type cast themselves with a single style or niche and instead lean towards generic design styles.

Another interesting contrast I found was that the smaller the group, the more prominent the sales pitch was. The larger shops seem to often rely on simply showing work on an epic scale while smaller organizations sell you on their process and particular skill set. I think this is makes sense. Larger shops with big-name clients can rely on a, "If it is good enough for them, it is good enough for me" mentality. After all, if a shop can do incredible work for Nike or any other mega corporation, they can likely handle my job of an equal or smaller scale.

Dig into the following examples and consider how the scale of each shop is reflected in the design. I think it is an important consideration as you create your own portfolio site or one for an agency. My suggestion is to simply stay true to what you are—don't try to look bigger then you are.

03/One Man Show

www.frootdesign.com

www.mickael-girault.fr

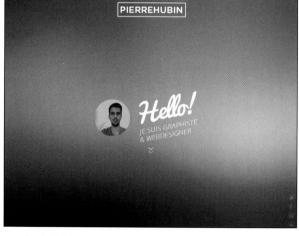

http://mattvojacek.com

www.pierrekarter.be

03/ The Micro Agency

(fewer than 10 people)

http://11beats.co.uk

www.higher.sk/en

www.enrichcreative.com

http://anthemdesignlab.com

03/Medium Agencies

(10 to 50 people)

http://integritystl.com

http://rno1.com

http://worryfreelabs.com

www.driftinteractive.com

03/Large Agencies

(50 people or more)

www.hugeinc.com

http://vladimirjones.com

www.bigspaceship.com

www.rga.com

04 /

PORTFOLIOS BY TYPE OF WORK

Another really interesting way to break down portfolio sites is by the type of work showcased in them. This is by no means an exact science due to the fact that many people do various types of work. As a result, many of the samples here would likely fit into many other niches. I did work hard to show examples that focus on the topic at hand. That said, I still feel it is really interesting to see how web designers in common fields have chosen to differentiate themselves.

In particular I think you will find some interesting ideas in the section filled with portfolios for non-design work (page 067). Here you will find examples from wide-ranging professions such as tattoo artist, barber, comedian and videographer. Each of these has a specific type of work to showcase and certain skills to highlight.

One of my favorite techniques for getting fresh ideas is to simply look outside my chosen field of work. In this section, you should find a wealth of ideas in each of the categories presented. My work falls under the user experience design bucket (page 052); so I found great inspiration in looking at how fine artists showcase their work (page 070). Interestingly there is a lot of common ground between these two chapters. I can't help but notice many small details that get me thinking about how I would approach my own portfolio.

Another section here that really catches my personal attention is the one for icon designs (page 058). Icons like the ones shown create a beautiful experience and it got me thinking about how I could utilize icons of the work I do. To me this perfectly demonstrates the point of my Idea Books. You can easily take ideas from designers in other specialties and use them to inspire your own work. As a result you can introduce fresh ideas that solve your problems instead of simply taking a "me-too" approach and running with the current trend.

04/Interactive and Web

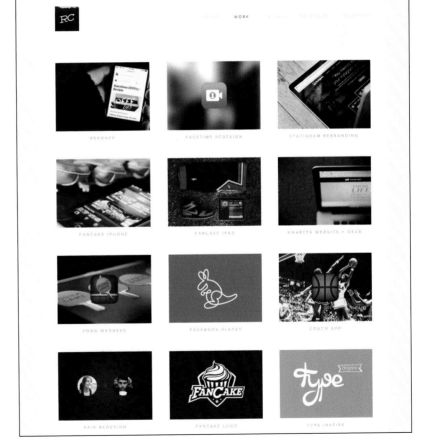

http://robinclediere.com

CLIENTS	FORMAT	WORK	MARKET	YEAR
Alliance Project	Mobile PDA Art	Flash	Art & Culture	2001
Agora	Mobile Application	Flash	Business Services	2004
American Board of Internal Medicine	Website	Visual Design	Healthcare	2006
American Express	Interaction Design	Design & Development	Financial Services	2001
AmerisourceBergen	Website	Flash Development	Healthcare	2007
Artisan Garden	Website	Flash	Consumer Services	2006
Barrett N Smith	Website	Flash	Arts & Culture	2006
Bixler's Jewelers	Website	Visual Design	Consumer Services	2010
Blessing Health System	Mobile	Visual Design	Healthcare	2011
Blue Mountain Health System	Website	Art Direction	Healthcare	2009
Born Magazine	Interactive Art	Flash	Art & Culture	2003
CASPA	Print	Art Direction	Healthcare	2003
Caretech Connectivity	Print	Flash	Healthcare	2010
Caretech Solutions Presentation	Application	Flash	Healthcare	2009
Carpenter Technology	Web Application	Visual Design	Business Services	2010
Cellphone Art - Start Mobile	Mobile Art	Flash	Art & Culture	2006
Centegra Health System	Website	Visual Design	Healthcare	2009
Checkpoint Systems	Print	Art Direction	Business Services	2003
Children's Discovery Institute	Website	Art Direction	Healthcare	2009
Children's Hospital of Philadelphia	CD-ROM	Art Direction	Healthcare	2005
Children's Hospital, New Orleans	Print	Art Direction	Healthcare	2007
Daytimere	Website	Art Direction	eCommerce	2001
Digitalwave	Website	Design & Development	Business Services	2002
Drexel Architecture	Presentation	Visual Design	Education	2009

BEAUTIFUL CAMPUS. BRIGHT FUTURE

LIVE IT.

Drexel Architecture Presentation

Information

Visual design and partial flash development for "Experience Drexel Architecture" Interactive Feature. Showcasing the history and architecture found on Drexel University's campus.

www.drexel.edu/architecture

Medium
Photoshop, Illustrator, Flash

CLIENTS	FORMAT	WORK	MARKET	YEAR
Drexel University	Website	Visual Design	Education	2008
Drexel University, Arts & Sciences	Website	Visual Design	Education	2008
Drexel University, College of Medicine	Website	Visual Design	Education	2008
Drexel University, Goodwin	Website	Visual Design	Education	2007
Elam Reavis	Print	Brand Identity	Consumer Services	2003
FLV Player	Application	Flash	Business Services	2002
Folksonomy Art	Art	Flash	Art & Culture	2010
Gecko9 Mobile	Mobile PocketPC	Flash	Art & Culture	2002

www.jonjon.tv

www.grondecki.pl

http://velthy.net

04/User Interface and User Experience Design

www.seanhermandesign.com

www.kylethacker.com

http://pavelhuza.com

www.leeannpica.com

04/Mobile App Design and Development

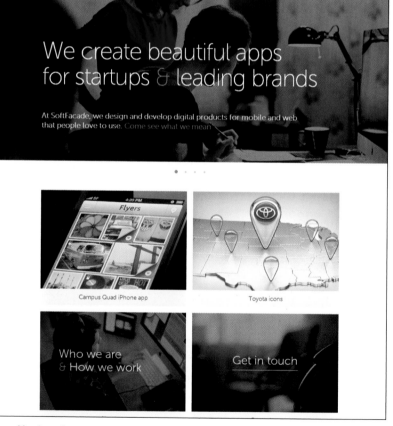

Campus Quad iPhone app

Toyota icons

www.softfacade.com/

http://fueled.com

http://kollectivemobile.com

http://attackpattern.com

04/ Developers and Programmers

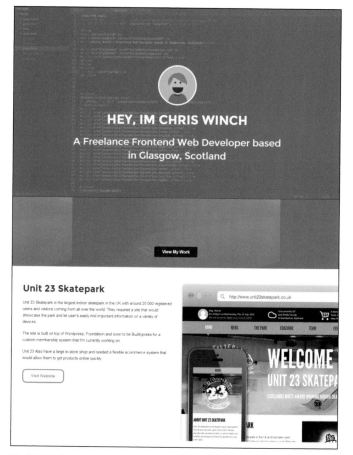

http://chriswinch.me

http://minimalmonkey.com

www.adhamdannaway.com

www.fogcreek.com

04/Icon Design

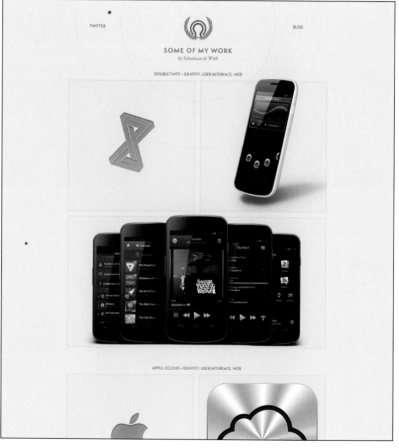

www.icondesigner.net

www.taylorcarrigan.com

www.midtonedesign.com

http://annapaschenko.com

04/Animation and Motion Graphics

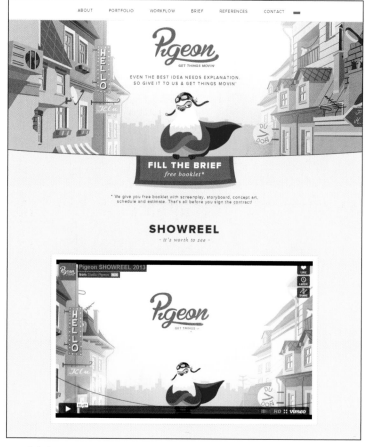

www.studiopigeon.com

www.oniric-creative.com

https://modio.tv

http://berd.tv

04/Branding and Logo Work

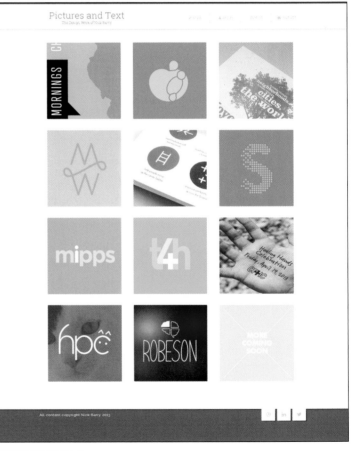

www.picturesandtext.co.uk

www.jeroenvaneerden.nl

www.helveticbrands.ch

www.werklig.com

04/Print Design

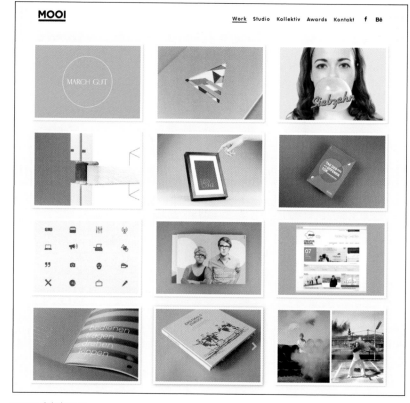

www.mooi-design.com

http://2xelliott.co.uk

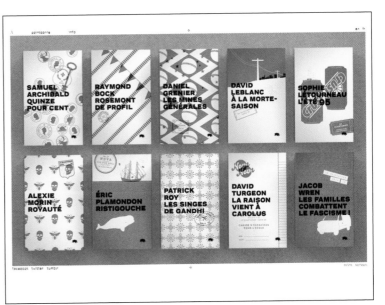

http://pointbarre.ca/en

www.moodley.at/de/willkommen.html

04/Typography

www.bmddesign.fr

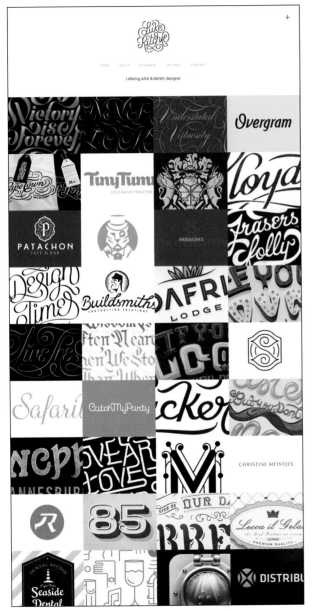

www.lukeritchie.co.za

www.rafagoicoechea.info

http://typefounding.com

04/Photography

www.timtadder.com

www.levonbiss.com

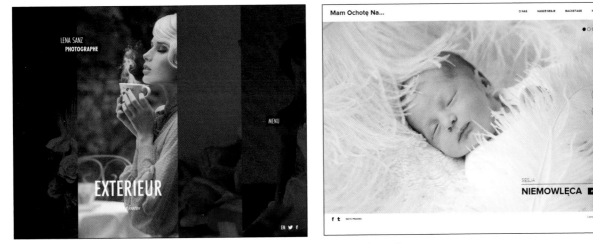

www.lena-sanz.com

http://mamochotena.pl

04/Fine Art

www.turksworks.co.uk

http://michalsawtyruk.com

www.jefflangevin.com

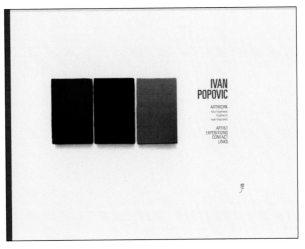

www.ivanpopovic.com

04/Illustration

www.visio-art.de

www.nabilnezzar.com

http://kerbyrosanes.com

www.beatrizsanches.com

04/Advertising

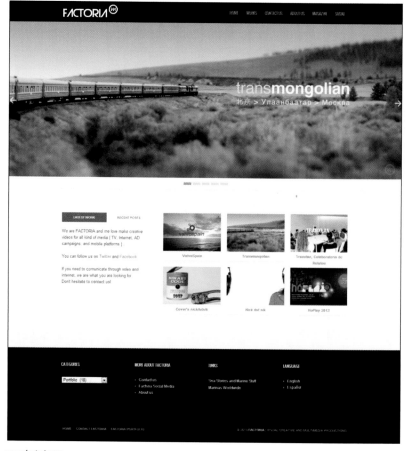

www.factoria.me

http://grey.com

www.rizon.be

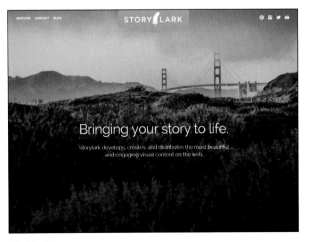

http://storylark.com

04/Other Types of Work

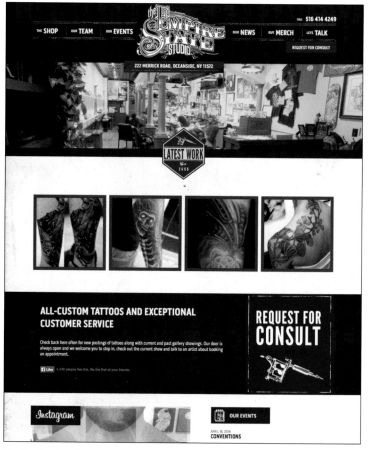

http://empirestatestudios.com

www.kenhoffa.com

www.davidfechner.de/barber

http://justweddings.ie

www.michellebuteau.com

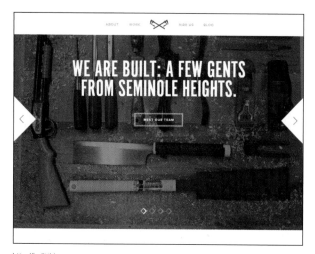

http://builtthings.com

http://parsons.me

www.mikecampau.com

05/

Flat Designs • Anti-Flat Design • 3-D Designs • Minimal •
Chromeless • White Text On a Photo • Vector-Style Illustrations •
Storytelling • The Super Hero • Chalkboards • Vertical Divides

DESIGN STYLES

Design styles tend to represent larger movements and patterns in the design world. Styles don't typically have specific elements associated with them, but rather are found in more of a common visual approach. These could be defined as overall theories in the approach to design. Minimalism is a prime example of how a type of design can drive what the artist produces. This style defines how it will look and feel, but doesn't create a formula for specific imagery, colors, type styles and so on. In contrast, designs sorted by themes do strike up specifics that can drive the overall direction of the design. The current love affair the world has with flat design is a perfect example of this. Carefully think through the style you select for your site and ensure that it plays into the overall brand and message of the site.

05/Flat Designs

I have mentioned flat design several times already in this book, sometimes in a negative manner. But don't get me wrong, the sites presented here are gorgeous, and frankly I would be happy if I could say I had designed any of them. The sites are beautiful and vividly display the style that is currently extremely popular. My biggest beef with this style is that it feels so generic at times. In many cases, you could take the logo off one site and slap it on any other flat design. With this in mind, I very carefully selected the set of sites you see here. In my opinion, these sites leverage the flat aesthetic, but do so in a way that avoids an overly generic result. The sites feel distinct and perfectly matched to the content.

Cotton Bureau **(FIGURE 1)** is a lovely example of this. The site clearly relies on a flat style and easily fits into the trendy design approach. And yet, there is nothing about the design that feels generic. Instead the design feels clearly connected to the product and style of the brand as a whole. They could have gone overboard with cotton and fabric textures. It would have been easy to justify and would have felt rather natural. Instead, they followed the visual style of the current age but with their own touches. For example, the pattern of t-shirts in the background helps give the site a unique visual twist.

I must caution though: Before you jump on the bandwagon with this style, be sure to think it through. Does the style resonate with the brand you need to showcase? Will it reinforce what the site needs to communicate? If so, the biggest question is: How can you tweak the style? What other style can you blend it with? How can you integrate the concept of your site with the design? In other words, what can you do to make your flat design different from all the other flat designs out there?

FIGURE 1: https://cottonbureau.com

www.namesforchange.org

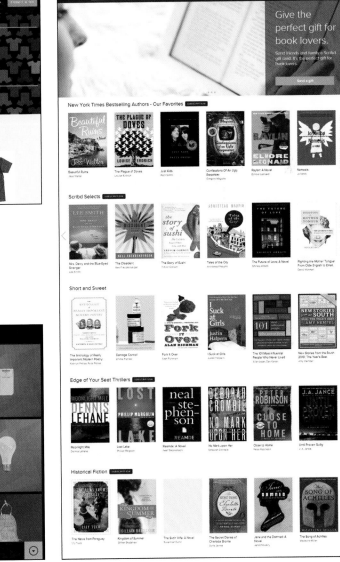

FIGURE 2: www.scribd.com

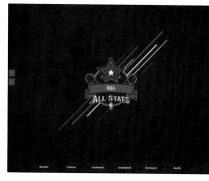

http://nballstats.com

www.meetingresult.com

http://poncho.is/register

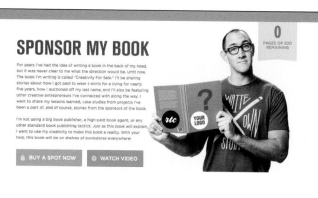

http://sponsormybook.com

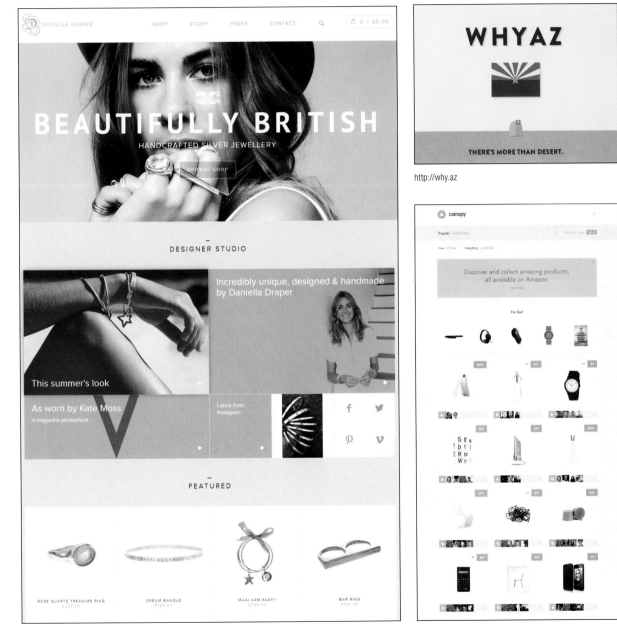

http://danielladraper.com

http://why.az

http://canopy.co

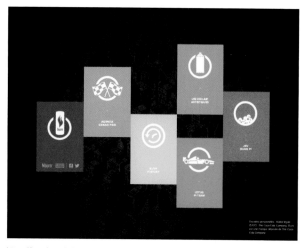

http://thezoomproject.com

https://burnformule1.com

www.prosperity.com

http://jims-scarf.co.uk

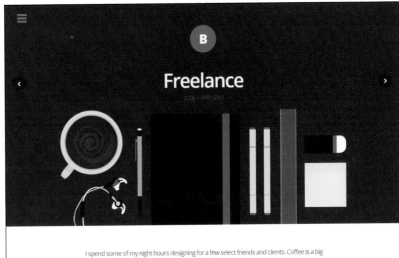

http://bradleyhaynes.com/freelance

https://pillpack.com

05/Anti-Flat Designs

Quite often flat design is described as the opposite of a skeuomorphic approach to design. Skeuomophic design is when a digital interface emulates its real world counter part. For example, a digital on/off switch that is made to look like a real world switch. This contrast between flat and skeuomorphism is most likely due to the evolution that has occurred on Apple devices. They are transitioning away from the skeuomorphic approaches Steve Jobs endorsed. While I understand the connection between these two styles, it is a contrast that makes the most sense in the world of native mobile apps and mobile operating systems. Look to the web and you will find that web designers very rarely rely on skeuomorphs—at least to the degree they did in previous versions of iOS.

This got me thinking: what is the real opposite of flat design? I have not-so-cleverly dubbed it anti-flat design. This approach doesn't rely on over-the-top skeuomorphs, but does manage to essentially ignore the flat style. The samples collected here have depth and visual richness that disconnects them from the flat and minimalistic styles quite vividly.

A fantastic example of this is the Maryland Brewers' Harvest website **(FIGURE 1)**. If you were to remove the various textures used in the site and substitute the dynamic decorative type with flat text, this example easily could have been flat. And yet it is not. As you consider the topic and content of the site, the visual richness they have opted for is perfect. It fits the organic colors and various textures we associate with beer—as seen in the imagery on the site.

Another example of this approach is the Dash site **(FIGURE 2)**. Again, this could have oh-so-easily been yet another flat design. Instead it has gradients (gasp!) and even some shadows (don't faint). I know, it is really shocking isn't it? Interestingly, the site relies on things that are shunned right now, and yet the site feels completely fresh and modern. I don't feel that it is dated or out of place at all. It feels perfectly natural and has a unique and beautiful style. After an overdose of flat design, the buttons do in fact feel more clickable, and the action items on the site feel just a bit more obvious.

As always, consider what you can take away from this. Perhaps the answer is to take an otherwise flat design and put a small touch of non-flat back into it. Through this the design takes on a fresh feel, and the action items can be extremely obvious. Frankly, this is pretty much what all of the examples here have done. They take the same overall feel of flat design and add a dash of anti-flat design back in.

FIGURE 1: http://mdbrewersharvest.com

FIGURE 2: www.thedash.com

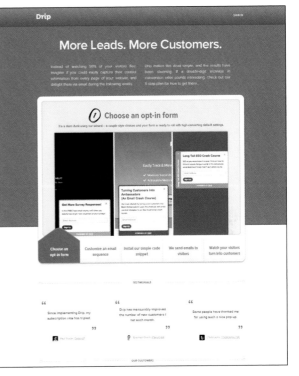

www.getdrip.com

www.tantefanny.at

http://good-morning.no/casestudies/good-morning-breakfast

www.pwdo.org/ffc-2013

www.localsapparel.se

www.athenos.com

www.rentalengine.com

http://cervezaaustral.cl/viajealorigen

https://spacebox.io

http://mailplaneapp.com

05/3-D Designs

The 3-D design style is another trend that has a bit of a anti-flat design feel to it. Before your mind gets carried away, I am not describing sites that make use of radical 3-D environments in which you move around. I am focused here on sites that make small use of the approach. For example, the Safebyte **(FIGURE 1)** site uses a very subtle effect in the background to create a small sense of dimension. The images are at an angle and have a shadow, so you feel they recede into the background. The depth-of-field effect plays a significant role in the style as well. The point here is that the site has a sense of depth—achieved through imagery—but it does not attempt to be overly three-dimensional in nature.

Another fun example is The Design Files Open House website **(FIGURE 2)**. Here a simple photograph is placed behind the content (a rather popular approach, as found in the White Text on a Photograph chapter on page 104). In fact, the home page is a series of photos that all support this dimensional effect. The site is incredibly minimal, and yet the careful use of beautiful photographs gives the site a unique sense of depth.

The Greats site **(FIGURE 3)** has a beautiful holiday-themed element at the top of the page. Here the overlap of the ornaments combined with the shadows below them creates a simple 3-D effect. The results are simple but beautiful and captivating.

Overlapping elements is such a simple way to create depth and can result in some gorgeous results. A lovely example is the G-Star RAW home page **(FIGURE 4)**. In cases like this you can get away with the user not being able to read the full text. This won't always work, but here it does beautifully. The site has a gorgeous illusion of depth.

A few years ago the web was bonkers over the use of parallax elements. Every now and again you still find it at work (and most often in brilliant ways). The usage on LaTabla-DeGisela.com certainly fits this description. The colored elements at the bottom move in a parallax way, which is further reinforced by the out-of-focus elements that enhance the notion of depth. The results are animated as you move the mouse around the screen. It is a simple detail, but one that catches your attention and draws you in.

The use of depth brings a sense of life to these otherwise streamlined sites. Again, it feels a lot like these would be classic flat designs, but the designer has added some vividly non-flat elements to give the sites a depth they would otherwise lack. The sites are unique, gorgeous and stand on their own as distinct styles and brands.

FIGURE 1: www.safebyte.com

FIGURE 2: www.thedesignfilesopenhouse.com

FIGURE 3: http://greatsbrand.com

FIGURE 4: www.g-star.com

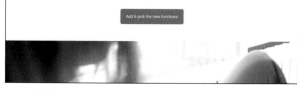

www.themobileindex.com

http://tablet.fubiz.net

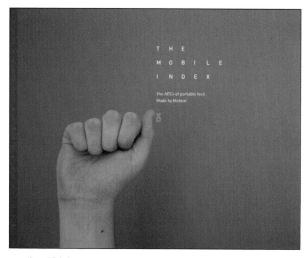

www.siaperitivos.com/en/home

http://one.htc.com/experienceit

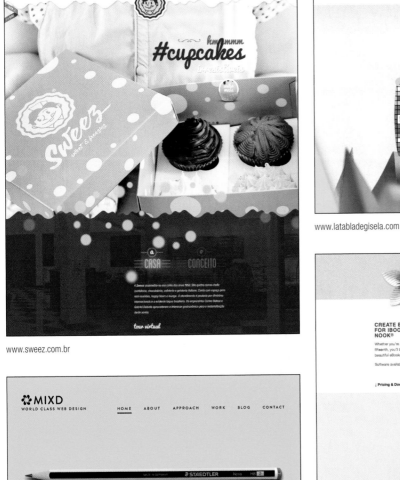

www.sweez.com.br

www.latabladegisela.com

http://180g.co/vellum

www.mixd.co.uk

05/Minimal

One of my favorite categories—one that has found its way into all of my Idea Books—is the minimal style. This style has been around for ages and has its roots clearly in the modern design movement, which of course easily predates the web. The work of Dieter Rams and his 10 principles of good design vividly communicate the principles at work in the sites shown here. I encourage you to read more about Dieter and his principles[1].

Consider one of Dieter Rams's principles: "Good design makes a product understandable." Think of this as you consider the IndMusic website **(FIGURE 1)**. The product this company offers is vividly clear and the minimalistic approach allows the clear value proposition to stand out. This approach can easily be found in many of the other examples as well, such as the Fiiinta website **(FIGURE 2)** or the Just Us site **(FIGURE 3)**.

Another of the principles states that "Good design is long-lasting." One could interpret this on the web as a timeless style that doesn't need to be updated simply because the visual aesthetic has changed. I think Howard Yount **(FIGURE 4)** embodies this perfectly. The site could have been made ten years ago, and I see no reason why it will feel out of date ten years from now. Except for the product they sell, the design of the site is timeless. Part of the reason for this leads me to the final principle I want to consider.

"Good design is as little design as possible" perfectly reflects the essence of the minimalist style. This is, in fact, one of the most effective ways to achieve a solid, long-lasting design that relies on very little supporting design, as we noticed on the Howard Yount site. As a result, the true beauty of this design is that it is both long lasting and minimalist in nature. I won't say it will be timeless forever, but many of the sites you would place in this category are close to that. The Molly & Me Pecans website **(FIGURE 5)** demonstrates this effectively. The site most certainly has as little as possible, and it is hard not to suggest that the design is timeless.

---

[1] Dieter Rams on Wikipedia: http://en.wikipedia.org/wiki/Dieter_Rams

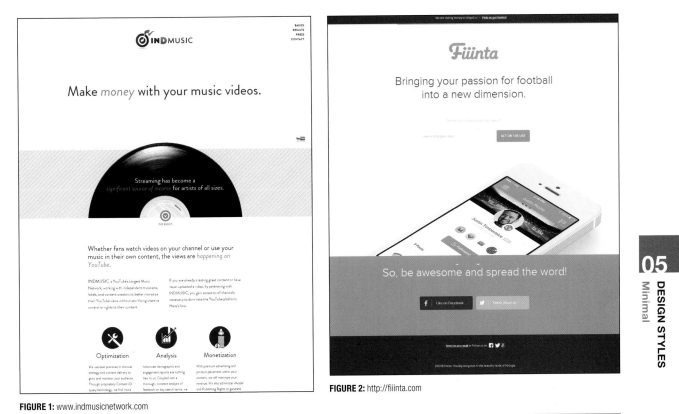

FIGURE 1: www.indmusicnetwork.com

FIGURE 2: http://fiiinta.com

FIGURE 3: www.justusdesigncollective.com

FIGURE 4: www.howardyount.com

FIGURE 5: http://mollyandmepecans.com

http://awbymary.com

http://madebyfriends.co/citibike

www.swissted.com

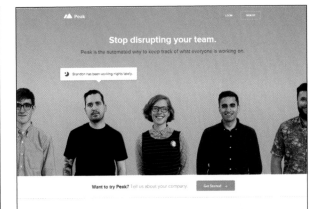

www.usepeak.com

http://siiiimple.eu.pn

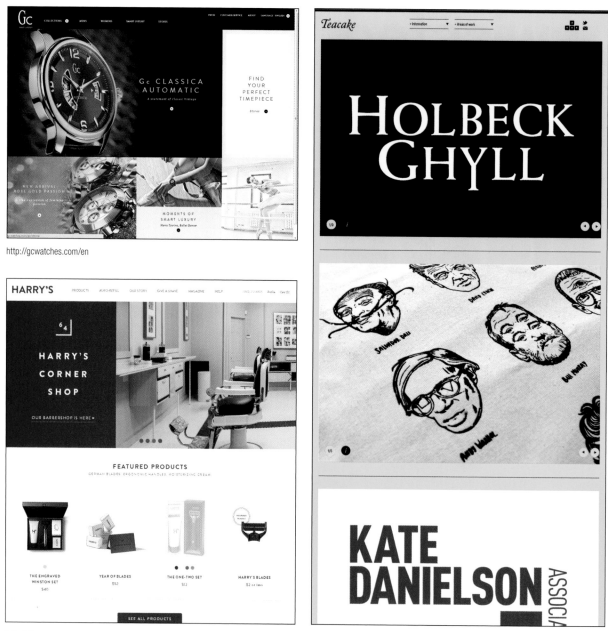

http://gcwatches.com/en

www.harrys.com

http://teacakedesign.com

www.cmyk-tower.com

www.dandad.org

http://openin.gs

05/Chromeless

This chapter follows the minimal one because as you will quickly see, they have a lot in common. In fact, this chapter is essentially a subsection of the minimal style. As usual, let's start by defining the style. Chromeless sites are those that are essentially void of any chrome, and by chrome I mean any sort of decorative containers. In the current web design trends it has become rather commonplace to avoid containers that frame content. Naturally, designers don't stick to this religiously, but it is still a common mentality. That said, the sites here make rather vivid use of the style and for the most part are completely void of any chrome.

A natural example that clearly shows its minimalistic roots is the Carrera Races site **(FIGURE 1).** The site of course is minimalist, but note that there is just a logo, navigation and content. There are no frames to contain things. This example is perhaps the simplest of the ones I have collected. For the most part, the rest of them rely on more complex visual styles where the lack of chrome is less noticeable. And though I believe the other sites could also be considered minimal, they are not what people typically think of when the minimal style comes to mind.

Take for example the TekRok **(FIGURE 2)**, the Hosoi Kaban **(FIGURE 3)** and Natalie Sklobovskaya's **(FIGURE 4)** sites. Though these sites essentially look nothing alike, they all lack the same element: structural decoration. The sites clearly do not lack in the area of style, and are each quite beautiful for their own reasons. But none of them rely on the structure of the site to create the beauty. Instead the focus is essentially on the content, so much so that pretty much anything that is not content has been removed. And though this description *sounds* like a minimalist style, I think you will agree when you view the screenshots that they are not your stereotypical minimal designs.

Some of the designs come really close to stepping beyond my definition of this style. For example The London Distillery site **(FIGURE 5)** has what might be considered chrome—the box of buttons, for example. However, I would argue that the buttons are the container, and therefore there is no container. It is for this reason that the style is somewhat elusive. At times it appears there is in fact a supporting structure that defines and decorates the layout. But as you focus on it more intently and break it apart you realize the content *is* the decoration. The results are a lovely step away from minimalism.

FIGURE 1: http://carreraworld.com/us

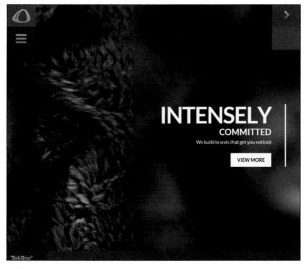

FIGURE 2: http://tekroc.com

FIGURE 3: http://kabanhosoi.com

FIGURE 4: www.sklobovskaya.com

FIGURE 5: www.thelondondistillerycompany.com

http://melanie-f.com

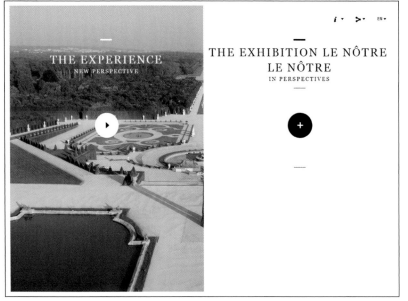

http://lenotre.chateauversailles.fr/entries_en.html

http://andy-wolf.at/onelove

www.reachpartners.ch

www.queenslandballet.com.au

http://museekly.com

http://appdock.co

05/White Text On a Photo

You know you're onto a popular trend when you define the topic, start collecting sites, and about five minutes later you have enough to fill a chapter. This is exactly the case with the trend of placing white text over a photograph. Most often the photos are stylized in some way so that the white text clearly pops out. Once you notice this, you will find this recipe at work in countless sites. I actually had to work hard to avoid putting too many sites with this formula throughout this book.

Some trends, like this one, are simply not as exciting and can often feel mundane, even useless. I would concur that if you simply use this because it is a visual approach that looks nice, it can become a crutch. Instead, I propose you keep it in mind as a useful formula to bust out when the time is right. Though it is simple—and seriously overused—this trend does have its useful points.

For example, the combination of text and image results in a set of supporting elements. Consider the Tiny Footprint Coffee **(FIGURE 1)** website. One quick look and you no doubt know exactly what the site is about. The image and text work together to create a cohesive message. This, to me, is the saving grace for this formula: the results can be very meaningful through a repeated message. Though coffee beans on a coffee site is a bit obvious, and probably way overdone, the results are beautiful and it is hard to argue with the clarity of purpose.

Another example I find to be particularly effective is the Curt's Special Recipe site **(FIGURE 2)**. Here the imagery isn't just some stylized stock photo—instead it is a shot of the actual product combined with some beautiful textures. The results are not only gorgeous, even yummy, but also extremely helpful to the design of the site. Again, the combined messages of the text and photos work to reinforce and drive home the point of the site. No confusion here.

What this approach can also do is set a clear tone for a site. Compare the Seattle Cider Co. site **(FIGURE 3)** with the Martina Sperl site **(FIGURE 4)**. Both use the same basic approach, and yet each has an extremely distinct feel. This is a very powerful approach that can really shape the feel of your site.

As with many trends, on the surface, this one is easy to discard. But as you dig in, I think you will find it is a rather effective tool. Just save it for the perfect scenario when it makes really good sense.

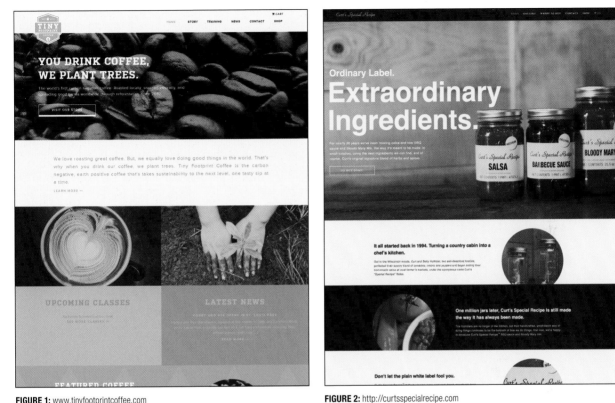

FIGURE 1: www.tinyfootprintcoffee.com

FIGURE 2: http://curtsspecialrecipe.com

FIGURE 3: www.seattlecidercompany.com

FIGURE 4: www.martinasperl.at

http://tribalmedia.co.uk

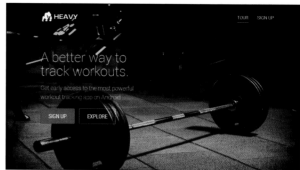

http://heavyapp.com

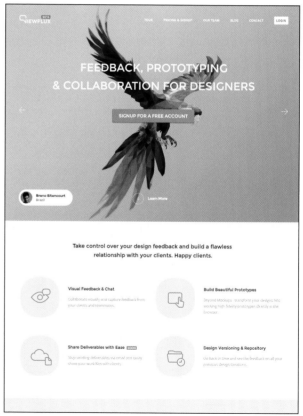

http://jellyreader.com

http://viewflux.com

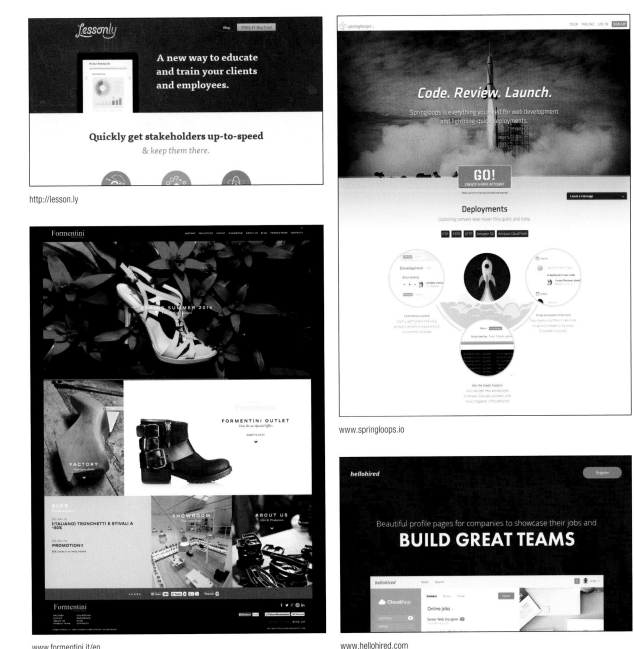

http://lesson.ly

www.springloops.io

www.formentini.it/en

www.hellohired.com

http://lifeandthyme.com

www.andremaurice.it

www.webuildrail.com

www.glasvasen.se

05/Vector-Style Illustrations

The use of illustrations in web design is something I have talked about for many years. As I reflect on it, I could easily create a timeline of various illustration styles the web has used over the years. These types of illustrations represent trends and tend to date a site. As you have likely guessed, the visual trend in illustration right now is toward a vector look and feel. A quick scan of the samples collected here demonstrates this. As with many of the trends in this book, you will notice this style in numerous other examples throughout this book.

I think the core reason this style started is because of the responsive web design movement. As designers started creating designs that could adapt to any screen size, they needed to put artwork with the designs. And if you want artwork that scales well, it only makes sense to use vector-oriented artwork. (Though ironically, an image of an illustration that is not vector-style will scale just as well. There literally is no difference.) Another aspect of the responsive movement was the rise of the flat design. This is most likely the second catalyst that drove this to be a popular style, as the results match really well with this other visual approach (check page 080 for more sites built with the flat style). As you will notice, many of the sites here make vivid usage of the flat style in combination with the vector illustrations.

As always, illustrations provide a way for designers to establish a unique visual style for a site. Even though all of the sites here use a similar basic approach, the results are truly diverse. One of my favorite examples is the Liberio artwork **(FIGURE 1)**. The device in the illustration sets the context for the product, but it does so in a fairly unique way. Rather than a photorealistic style that would match countless other sites, they relied on a stylized version that gets the point across.

Another example that I really love is the Battle of the Sexes site **(FIGURE 2)**. In a case like this, it is hard to imagine the site without the unique illustrations. Even if the site had a more typical structure, the illustrations really create a unique feel. And given the topic, it would be easy for this to fall apart. Instead, the unique vector-style illustrations give the site an appeal it would otherwise completely lack. The illustrations bring it to life and make it interesting.

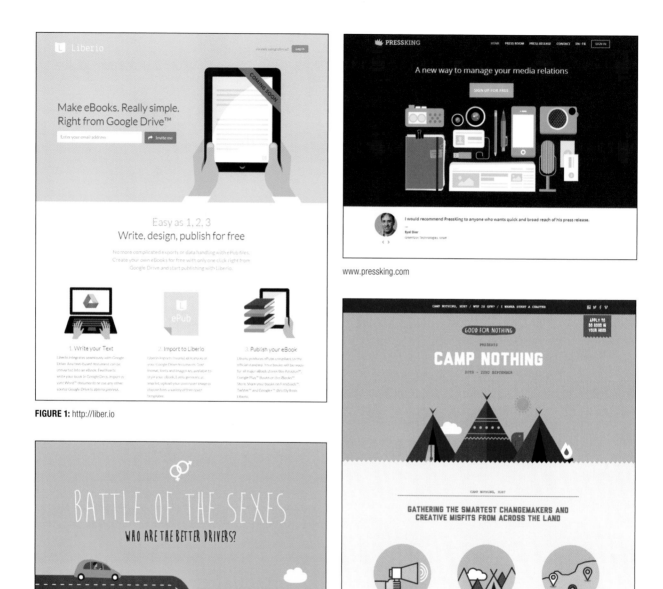

FIGURE 1: http://liber.io

FIGURE 2: https://towncentrecarparks.com/battle-of-the-sexes

www.pressking.com

http://campnothing.goodfornothing.com

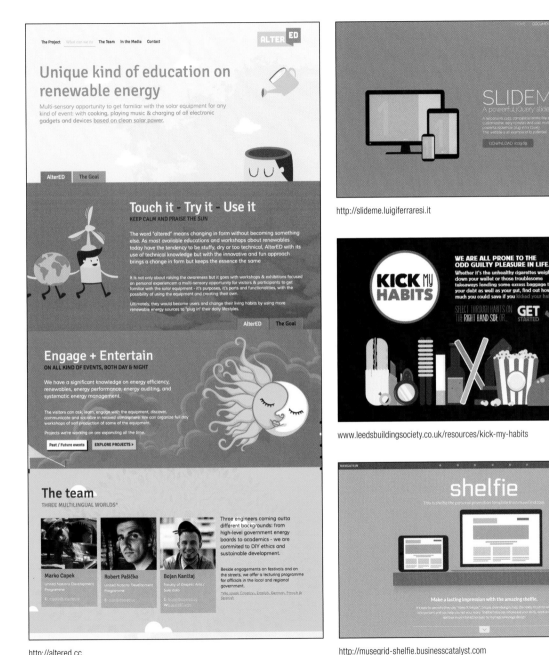

http://altered.cc

http://slideme.luigiferraresi.it

www.leedsbuildingsociety.co.uk/resources/kick-my-habits

http://musegrid-shelfie.businesscatalyst.com

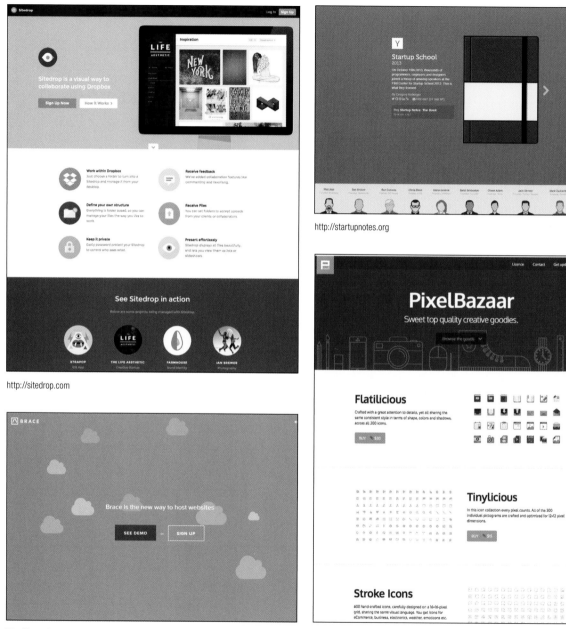

http://sitedrop.com

http://brace.io

http://startupnotes.org

www.pixelbazaar.com

05/Storytelling

A shift that has been happening in web design for some time now is from a static informational format to more of a storytelling approach. Though it is obviously not universal, some sites avoid just presenting the facts, and instead weave a more interesting and compelling story around the product.

Great examples of this can be found on many software websites. In some cases the actual product is not so obvious, though the story the site presents is targeted at capturing a specific audience's attention. Naturally the people they seek to captivate are their target audience to buy the software. Rather than start with screenshots and feature lists, many applications lead in with a story of some sorts.

Perhaps it is obvious, but in most cases the story is not over the top, but rather established with a tiny bit of mystery. In contrast, most of the samples collected here create storytelling approaches in a far more extreme way. They go about this in different ways, but together the results tell an interesting story about the trend.

All of the examples here are great and well worth a visit, but a few do stand out to me. First up is ContextAd **(FIGURE 1)**. This beautiful site is yet another online advertising outlet. They used a story-like approach to help dispel assumptions about the product and to help clarify the need for their distinct service. It's a storytelling approach, but ultimately it is really a sales pitch.

Another example that is really interesting to me is the OgilvyOne Big Data site **(FIGURE 2)**. Let's be honest, big data is not an exciting topic. In order to make it interesting, compelling and ultimately successful this site uses a very clear story-based approach to present the site's core message. And guess what? They made a really boring topic engaging and interesting.

Finally, this minisite from Golden Submarine **(FIGURE 3)** uses a story-based structure to sell them as a solid web agency. Essentially the story seeks to establish them as experts in their field. In this case it works really well. In the sea of portfolio sites I reviewed for this book, I have to admit that this one caught my attention. In fact, I was determined to leave agency and portfolio sites out of the rest of this book due to the dense set of them at the front, but this one was just too beautiful to pass up (I am such a sucker for gorgeous web design.)

FIGURE 1: www.freeger.com/projects/contextad

FIGURE 3: http://whaternet.com

www.f-i.com/fi/airlines

FIGURE 2: http://adayinbigdata.com

ADIEU, MES AMIS.

Taking care of your secrets was an exciting assignment. But times have changed and today, with new systems approaching, I'm no longer needed.

As I always say, security begins with your attitude, so please stay alert and don't rely on technology only. Enough said. Let's not get sentimental, but I will miss you somehow.

À bientôt,
Benoît

We kept the mean streets alive.
Want to take a walk with ben?

ENTER THE MEAN STREETS

http://benthebodyguard.com

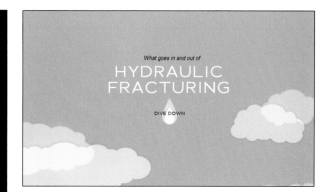

www.dangersoffracking.com

http://doyouimpress.com

http://futureofcarsharing.com

www.uppercup.com.au

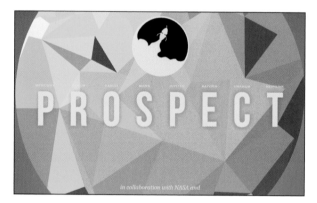

http://nasaprospect.com

www.welldoneteamgb.com

http://startupsthisishowdesignworks.com

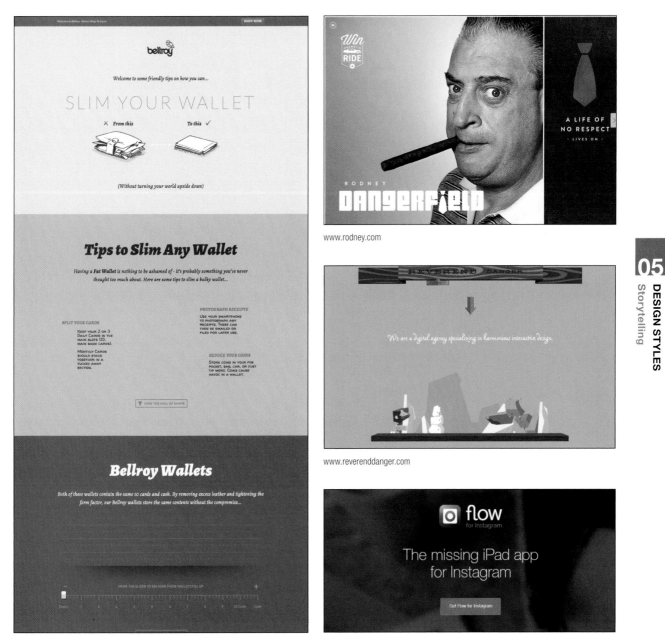

http://bellroy.com/pages/slim-your-wallet

www.rodney.com

www.reverenddanger.com

www.theflowapp.com

05/The Super Hero

The almighty content slider has been a go-to element for web designers over the last four years or so. At times it seemed like a timeless element that would be around forever. And though we still find it at work on many home pages, it seems that this particular element is losing traction. In its place, we find that a new home page leader element is finding its way into countless designs. I lovingly refer to it as the Super Hero. Those in marketing are likely familiar with the typical "hero shot." The alcohol industry is notorious for these with their super-sized and nearly glamorous shots of liquor bottles. The format I am referring to here is a situation where the home page is dominated by a hero section that summarizes a product. Noticeably gone is the content slider offering up multiple perspectives on the same product. Instead, we find a single super-sized section with the most succinct positioning possible for the product.

An absolutely perfect demonstration of this is the Goldee site **(FIGURE 1)**. Here we find a single large image of the product, a three-word summary of what it does and a call to action to get your own. You will also no doubt notice the large button in the middle of all this that allows you to watch a video of the product. This super hero section, were it made a few years ago, would have likely been a slider with about four frames, each frame showing some aspect of the product that makes it super cool.

I would propose that in many cases, the content slider is a crutch that allows designers to appease many people involved in a product. It lets them highlight many aspects of a product, each perhaps from a different person's perspective. Imagine how the following people might want to market a product differently: the CEO, marketing, developers, designers and so on. Each might think a different aspect is the best way to sell it. The end result is a muddled mess that works harder than it should. Instead the super hero approach works to find the single best and most concise sales angle. The results are simpler to use, easier to maintain, and just feel better for the consumer. As you noticed on the Goldee site, the video is the more full-blown sales pitch. But rather then put it front and center, they make you click to get it. As such, you aren't forced into it if you don't need it. If you're tired of the worn out content slider, give the super hero a chance.

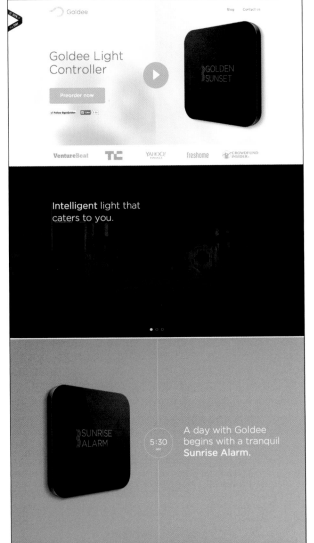

FIGURE 1: http://getgoldee.com

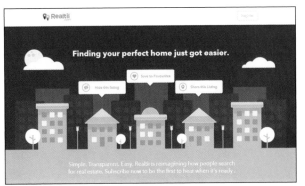

http://realtii.com

www.pinkanova.com/en

http://wondergiant.com

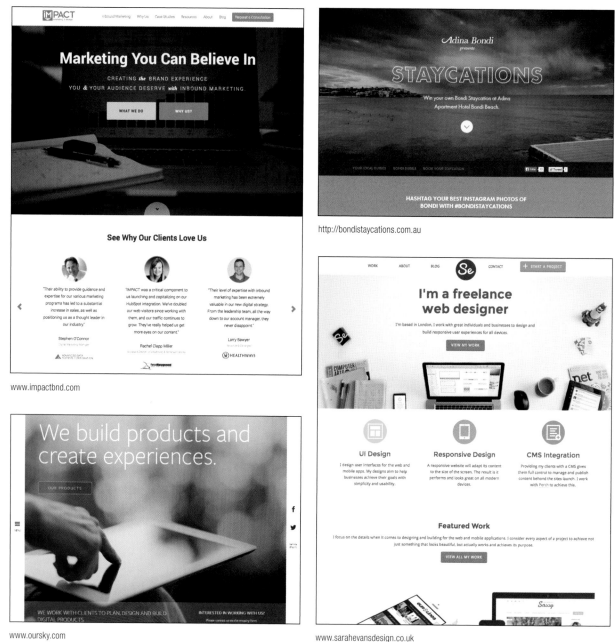

www.impactbnd.com

http://bondistaycations.com.au

www.oursky.com

www.sarahevansdesign.co.uk

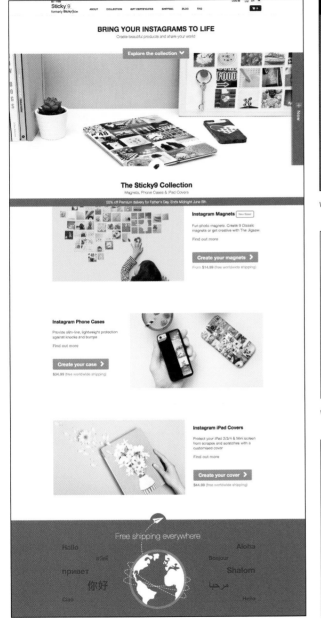

https://stickygram.com

www.thebentbullet.com

www.thezebra.com

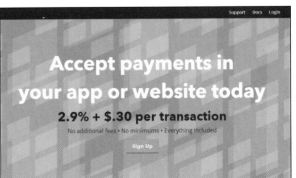

www.braintreepayments.com

https://squareup.com

www.audreyazoura.fr

www.boldking.com

http://procreate.si

05/Chalkboards

Though this book, as with all of my books, tries to focus on the most popular trends and styles, there are at times styles and approaches that get used by multiple people, but are somehow far less commonplace. This chapter is just such a situation. Though I have collected eight sites that rely on a chalkboard theme or element, it is not a pervasive style. If you look into print design you will find that the chalkboard theme is obnoxiously popular and it seems that almost every last magazine has taken a turn at applying the style to their cover, from *O, The Oprah Magazine* to *Time* magazine and countless publications in between[1]. I had previously noticed this style in print as I prepared lessons regarding editorial design for the graphic design program where I teach. When I spotted the style in the web world, I presumed it was equally popular. Much to my surprise there were but a few samples to find. I actually doubted for a while that I would have enough to create a chapter here. That said, I am happy to have filled this chapter and perhaps spark some new ideas. Frankly, it always feels good to highlight some lesser used styles and trends.

This particular style manifests itself in a variety of ways, the most common of which is as a background element. A prime example of this is the personal site of Carmen Rose **(FIGURE 1)**. Here the element is essentially a decorative element that contributes to a hip and stylish design. I suspect that this is perhaps a photograph of the photographer's studio. If so, it not only decorates the site but also serves as a sort of landmark for the artist and her space. It is an interesting way of connecting reality with the website. On a side note, this sort of glimpse into the reality of an artist is a really great way to minimize the technical aspect of the web and drive the focus toward the human side. It is a rather effective tool to communicate the mood and the tone of the site (and therefore those behind the site).

In other cases, such as with the BootBe website **(FIGURE 2)**, we find that the element is more than a simple background. Here the content is rendered as part of the chalkboard. In this way the element takes on a much more thematic approach. It is really interesting to contrast these two examples and see how such a vividly defined element as this can still take on numerous roles in a design.

---

[1] A Google image search to prove the point: http://bit.ly/1a2z5vU

FIGURE 1: http://lovecarmenrose.com

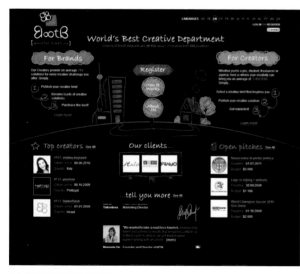

FIGURE 2: www.bootb.com/en

http://poppiesflowers.com.au

www.heritagechickens.ca

www.pastini.com

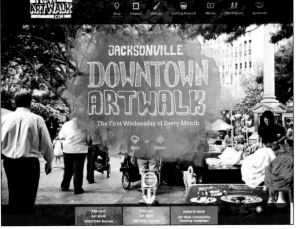

http://jacksonvilleartwalk.com

http://colabwork.com

http://nativesunjax.com

05/Vertical Divides

As I collect the examples used in my books, I browse many thousands of sites (yes, thousands). It takes a remarkable amount of work to collect the sites you find here. In fact, I would suggest that collecting the samples is at least 80 percent of the overall work. Along the way I can't help but notice a few lesser used approaches. Sites that make use of a center vertical divide are an example of this. Probably 75 percent of the way through collecting sites I realized I had seen quite a few sites doing this. I finally decided to make a chapter out of it. As a result, I scoured the web and my database of sites to collect the examples you see here. Perhaps this makes me sound a bit nuts; at a minimum it highlights the obsessive nature these books support.

As I observe the sites in this category, it strikes me that having a perfectly centered divide in a design is not the most likely of things. Given the horizontal nature of computer screens it isn't the easiest design format to choose. For this reason I personally find it to be an interesting and inspiring approach. It fascinates me to see how various designers have used the structure, as shown here. You will no doubt notice that I also squeezed in a few examples that don't quite fit the perfect 50/50 divide.

In some cases, such as the Wevseen site **(FIGURE 1)**, the divide separates what appears to be two equal elements of content. Neither seems to have the priority in the design. On first look I couldn't imagine that this was legit. After all, something just *has* to be more important. Then I remembered the site The News **(FIGURE 2)** that also features two perfectly equal chunks of content. It seems that in some isolated cases two pieces of content genuinely do have equal weight. A perfect split is a logical solution to this.

What I didn't expect to find was sites with this divide where the two sides of content scroll independently. However, such is the case with the Reveillon Absoluto site **(FIGURE 3)**. Visit this site and you will find that the content in the two sides is independent of the other side. Frankly, this seems rather bizarre and really confusing. But given the content and the purpose of the site, it actually really works. I love how this challenges my assumptions and gets me thinking in ways I would have never considered.

FIGURE 1: www.wevseen.com

FIGURE 2: http://thenews.im

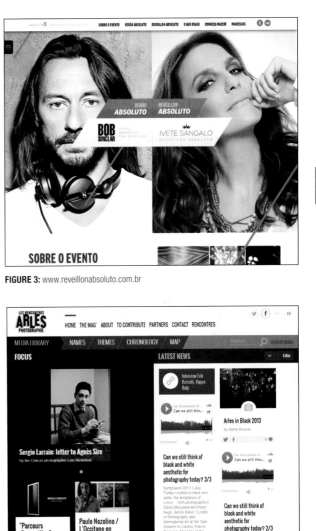

FIGURE 3: www.reveillonabsoluto.com.br

http://rencontres-arles-photo.tv/en

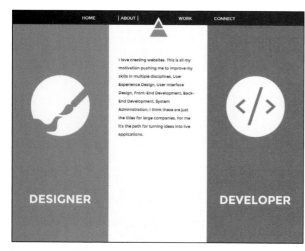

http://ahmetsulek.com

www.colehaan.com/wingtip-or-saddle.html

http://pakadlabezdomniaka.pl

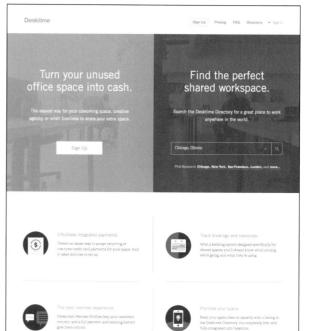

www.desktimeapp.com

www.newvision-opticien.com

http://eightandfour.com

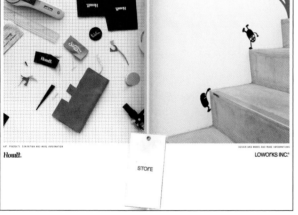

www.loworks.co.jp

www.fifty-five.com

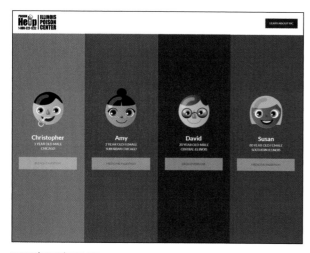

www.poisoncenterapp.com

http://instastox.com

www.avonesestilorcn.com/concurso/quintafase

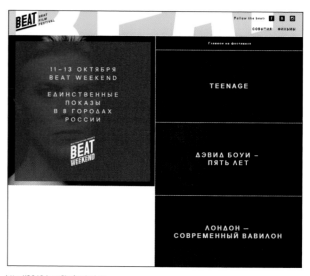

http://2013.beatfilmfestival.ru

06/

Monochromatic Plus One • Rainbow of Colors • Nature • Sketchy •
Vintage • Extreme • Futuristic • Holiday Branding

DESIGN THEMES

Themes and styles are closely related, but there is a difference. When it comes to themes there are specific visual elements and patterns that are easily connected to any given theme. It should also be noted that themes can be subtly woven into a site, or it can be completely over-the-top and dominate the entire design. A perfect example is the sketchy style. Once you settle on this as an approach, you drive yourself toward a specific type of visual. Sure there is a lot of latitude in that space, but the theme locks you in. Contrast this with something like a minimalist *style*. In that case there is no visual language that is prescribed other than the basic philosophy of the style. Themes can be a really fun design direction, leading to an almost infectious trail of ideas.

06/Monochromatic Plus One

Another style that is a sort of subset of the flat style is reducing the color palette to variations of a single color with one vivid contrasting color (almost universally white). This style runs the risk of being rather generic. The upside is that, for the most part, each of the sites here using the style have an extremely narrowed focus. This focus is further reflected in the minimalist color palette. There is just something about it that works really well. It allows the singular function of the sites to shine.

A few of the examples demonstrate this in a rather extreme way, doCapture **(FIGURE 1)** and Font Awesome **(FIGURE 2)** in particular. These sites have a very simple purpose and essentially one thing to offer to the world. As such, the super tight color palette and clear structure of the page reflects this simplicity. It really is an amazingly beautiful and effective approach. The Font Awesome site packs as much style as possible into the little bit of content that the site ends up with a really unique style, despite its minimalist approach.

I think this is a style that can be underestimated in terms of difficulty. If you don't put the extra work into it, your results *will* be generic. You have to work hard to add the extra details and touches that make your design unique. Anyone can take a solid color and slap some text on it. So what can you do to make it unique and give it the pop it needs? It seems that in this case, the devil truly is in the details.

If you have scanned the samples here you no doubt noticed that one of the sites stands out as a misfit: the Zegna site **(FIGURE 3)**. This site doesn't quite fit this style perfectly, but I included it here nonetheless. One of my favorite things about trends in general is to see how you can take one and push it just beyond what it is expected. This site is essentially black and white using a single accent color (gold tones). Black and white isn't quite the monochromatic style you see in the other samples, but it does come close. What I love is that the site feels full color, and yet it has a very narrow palette of colors. I think this is a clever and gorgeous use of the style. I know that I seldom consider creating a narrowed color palette when photographs of objects are involved. And yet the results are just amazing.

FIGURE 1: http://skakunmedia.com/docapture

FIGURE 2: http://fontawesome.pro

FIGURE 3: www.zegna.com/us

http://throttleapp.me

www.breakitdown.ie

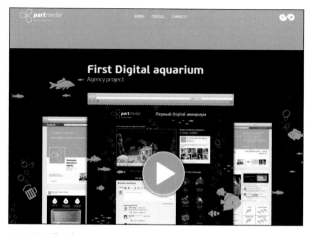

www.partmedia.ru/en

www.3coasts.com

www.vgrafiks.com

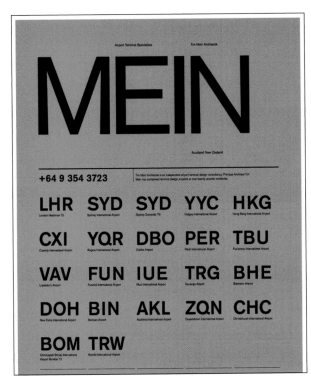

www.terminalplanning.aero

www.huxtaburger.com.au

www.getuikit.com

www.runthegap.com

06/Rainbow of Colors

A side effect of the flat pixel design craze has been a reduction in the variety of color we find in layouts. It seems that a monochromatic mentality has become the norm. As such, the sites presented here tend to stand out. These sites simply rely on a much wider range of colors. Naturally, they do so in a wide variety of ways. But most of them have used color variety as an aspect of the fundamental design of the site and not just in the content.

A great example to start with is this international site Beebeebazaar **(FIGURE 1)**. As you will notice, the site does indeed rely on a rainbow of colors. What I appreciate about this example is that it uses a wide variety of colors while avoiding two obvious paths. For starters, it doesn't feel like the stereotypical rainbow. Instead, it simply feels colorful. Don't pigeonhole this style as one that must feel like a bright intense rainbow. Secondly, the site doesn't feel kid-like. One of the most annoying limitations of the full-blown rainbow style is that it inevitably has a kid-like feel to it. Here you will notice the color palette feels vibrant and alive; it feels refreshing and fun. Yet it still feels professional and designed. It's a lovely demonstration of the style.

In stark contrast, the Carrefour Kid's Club site **(FIGURE 2)** pretty much fulfills the stereotypes I had in mind (and I suspect you can easily relate). That said, it works really well. If you seek to engage children, I can testify to the effectiveness of this approach. At the time of this writing my children are 2 and 5 and I can affirm that this simply works; it is easy to observe the site's appeal to my children. As such, in cases like this it makes good sense to leverage a stereotype. If it works, why fight it?

An interesting middle ground can be found at work on the Drishti website **(FIGURE 3)**. Though the site uses a typical rainbow of colors, it somehow doesn't feel like a rainbow. It just feels colorful. And though the color palette might resonate with children, the site avoids this by going with a modern design. Aside from the illustration, the design feels more adult. The end results are an interesting mix of the benefits of this style.

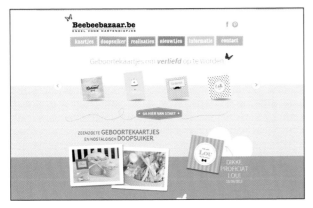

FIGURE 1: www.beebeebazaar.be

FIGURE 2: www.carrefourkidsclub.fr

FIGURE 3: http://cetdrishti.com

http://beurreandsel.com

www.gridbooks.com

www.triplagent.com

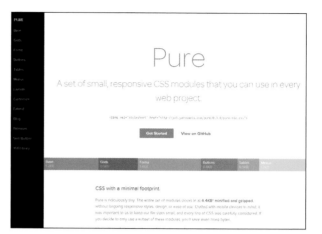

http://purecss.io

http://websites-for-artists.com

www.minttwist.com

www.freelancelift.com

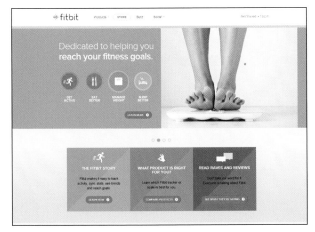

www.fitbit.com

http://giphy.com

06/**Nature**

Some themes are what I consider more extreme than others, and the nature theme is one of them. As you can see from the examples here, you can make a more subtle use of it. But all the same, the nature theme is one that tends to lead to more extreme results.

A perfect example of this is the Cups site **(FIGURE 1)**. Here the theme completely defines the entire design of the site. It isn't a supporting element, it *is* the design. In this case, it works well and turns an otherwise slightly boring topic into an interesting one. But notice that the theme isn't mindlessly applied. There is a connection to the content that is meaningful and ensures that the style of the site reinforces the message. It isn't a useless decoration. The site works to help others learn to help themselves. With people learning to fish the nature theme works really well and plays into a commonly known idea.

In other cases, the theme is far simpler. Take the Bonfire coming soon page **(FIGURE 2)** for example. Here it isn't so much a theme as a simple photograph. All the same, the photo plays into the feel of the site and the general vibe you get from it. The nature photo connects with the brand name and primarily serves as a decorative element.

At times a theme is almost handed to you. As an example, look at the Tillamook minisite **(FIGURE 3)**. This site represents a dairy farm that produces cheese. The nature theme is kind of obvious. In this case, the illustration style they used for the theme helps the site stand out. Best of all it avoids cliché images of cows or blocks of cheese.

If you are working on a design and it simply isn't coming to life, you should consider an extreme theme. It is by no means a universal solution. But if you are working with something dull, a theme like this can be a fantastic way to make it fun again. Let's face it, if you the designer are bored with it, the intended audience is even more likely to be bored. After all, you're being paid to look at it; the audience will be much less tolerant. Themes are a really fun way to breathe life back into an otherwise lifeless design.

FIGURE 1: www.cupsannual.ca

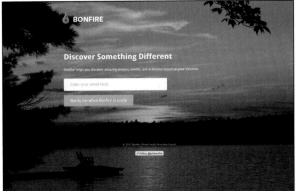

FIGURE 2: http://joinbonfire.com

FIGURE 3: www.tillamook.com/tillamook-story/our-story.html

http://cclfuture.org

www.zanggroeptimeless.nl

http://buryyoursecrets.se/en

www.annapurnarecruitment.com

www.nutcache.com

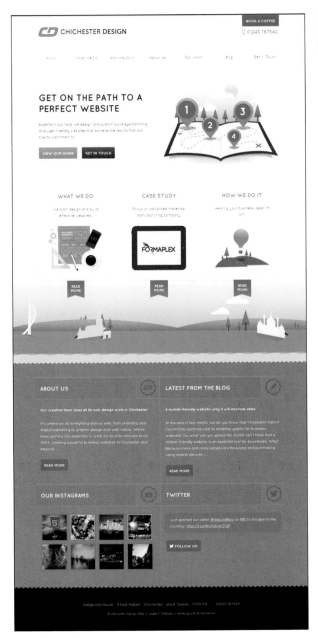

http://chichesterdesign.co.uk

www.shiner.com

www.globeview.nl

http://caitlinwicker.com

06/Sketchy

The use of sketchy design elements on the web is a trend I fully expect to stand the test of time. As an illustration style, it is a natural option that comes with some interesting nuances, and these nuances can be put to good work in many ways. A prime reason to use this approach is to simply break the trap of the digital realm. By this I mean that we can help people forget they are using digital media and create something that feels more organic and natural. One reason to this that I see over and over is to disconnect with some stereotype of being overly technical: Render something in a sketchy way and it will simply feel more approachable.

A good example to start with is Fruux **(FIGURE 1)**. This contact, calendar and tasks utility uses a sketchy style for the home page illustrations. Sure it looks nice, but that isn't reason enough to use a style—somehow, the style actually gives the impression that the software will be easy to use. It doesn't look technical and complicated. The sketchy style implies that it will be easy. I know the trick, and yet I can't help but think that the app really must be dead simple to use.

Most online maps are vector-style illustrations that seem straightforward, even if they contain some unique colors or artwork. The map found on this Greenpeace minisite **(FIGURE 2),** however, feels nothing like that. Instead it uses rich textures and alludes to a sketchy style. Ironically, it is barely hinting at the sketch and rough lines; they are nearly perfect, with only a few subtle variations. And the lines on the map are clearly based on vector paths and not hand-rendered lines. Even with these more polished parts, the design feels sketchy and organic. As a result the map evokes a different mood. I will leave you to speculate on the purpose of the design as it relates to the site; I know for me it feels like a reasonable and effective pairing.

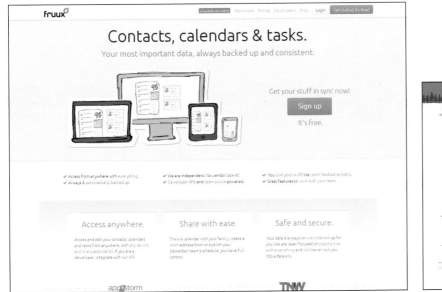

FIGURE 1: https://fruux.com

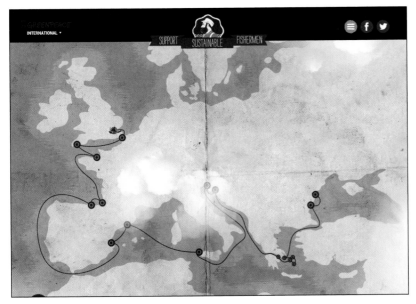

FIGURE 2: http://myboat.gp/en

http://4pinesbeer.com.au

http://candccoffee.com

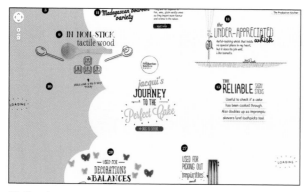

http://jacquico.com

http://packdog.com

www.adline.ro

www.served-mcr.com

http://chalkythecat.com

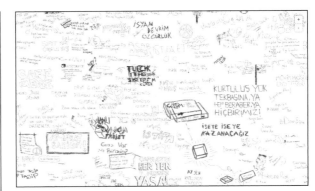

http://direnduvar.com

www.kezjukebox.com

www.numero10.ch/fr

06/Vintage

In the past, retro design was connected to a particular over-the-top style. This is something I featured in my first Idea Book. Look at the designs there and you will see some rather extreme theme-based sites. Fast forward to Volume 3 and you will find a section on 19th-century design where the sites weave in elements from that time period. In this chapter, which I am titling Vintage, I want to feature sites that fit the modern format and structural style—the twist being that they are decorated and styled using type, imagery and colors with a vintage feel to them. In a few cases the theme is a bit more extreme than others, but generally speaking, the approach is more subtle and woven into what are otherwise very normal sites. Missing here are overly thematic interfaces that rely on quirky retro elements to get users to engage with the content.

A lovely example to start with is S's vintage fashion website (**FIGURE 1**). It would be tempting for such a product line to get really carried away with making a vintage site. Fortunately, the designers thought better, and we find a site that fits the modern age. The type and color all feel very much at home on the modern web, but these elements have a vintage feel to them—a dated look that connects with the products in a more subtle way. I find the results to be amazing and the end product feels much higher-end than a more retro style might have resulted in.

Others, like the Tradestone Confections (**FIGURE 2**) site, the Wootten site (**FIGURE 3**) and the HAG (**FIGURE 4**) site are perhaps even a bit more subtle. With understated textures and carefully selected colors and fonts, the results are visibly vintage. If I could, I would do a whole book of sites in this style, as many are simply gorgeous. These sites need not rely on overly thematic designs to get the point across, and doing so would only serve to cheapen the design.

In contrast, a few of the sites, like The Peanut Gallery (**FIGURE 5**) and Stall & Dean (**FIGURE 6**) use far more striking and thematic elements. The approach is more heavy-handed, but overall effectively merges with modern takes on various design elements. Frankly, the sites are a breath of fresh air in a web world so narrowly focused on flat designs void of decoration. These sites suddenly feel rich, ornate and dramatic with such a contrast of styles.

FIGURE 1: http://stiinas.myshopify.com

FIGURE 2: http://tradestoneconfections.com

FIGURE 3: http://wootten.com.au

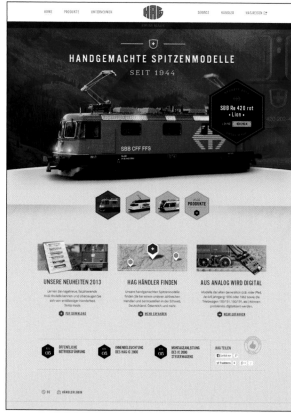

FIGURE 4: www.hag.ch/de

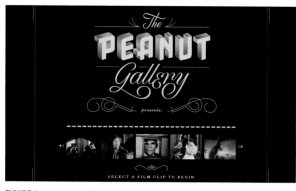

FIGURE 5: www.peanutgalleryfilms.com

FIGURE 6: www.stallanddean.com

http://connary.com/

http://milkeverymoment.ca

http://pulpfingers.com

www.mustasj.no

www.sweez.com.br

www.kinderfotografie-evihermans.be

06/**Extreme**

Extreme is the term I use to describe themes that are more than a small aspect of a design. In many cases the extreme theme takes over the entire design process and transforms everything into a thematic element. Due to the ultraconservative nature of flat design, the benchmark for an extreme theme is much lower than normal. Generally speaking, themes like this have fallen out of popularity, though not entirely out of use. I imagine that as with all things this will change over time as designers shift back toward more literal styles.

A perfect demonstration of this is the Pigeon site **(FIGURE 1)**, which relies on a pigeon theme. The design isn't based on an immersive, thematic experience where you navigate literal elements of the theme. Instead, it relies on artwork and language that reflects the theme. The design strikes a nice balance between thematic design and ease of use. The site's navigation and content are perfectly accessible and the theme serves as a layer of decoration to bring it to life. I think this is a real key to embrace: Don't sacrifice the usability of your website for the sake of theme. Once the theme starts getting in the way, you need to dial it back a bit as the sites here have done.

The PNC Gift Maker site **(FIGURE 2)** is perhaps the most extreme of the sites presented here. In this interface, the theme entirely takes over and there is little about this that feels normal. The design and interface harkens back to the era of Flash-based websites. But in this case, the entire creation has been crafted with good old-fashioned HTML and CSS. This is an example of when taking a theme to the extreme is a good thing. It can be risky, but the results can be amazing. When I say risky, I mean that the results can be painful to use. This site, however, is super easy and very intuitive. It is clear they made it a priority to ensure that people could easily use the wacky creation that they came up with.

In other examples like Jamcouver **(FIGURE 3)** and Cuisines Schmidt **(FIGURE 4)**, we find that the theme has been woven into structures and interface elements in a comfortable way. In fact, you could replace many of the extremely thematic elements with flat ones and have a site that functions quite well under a different style. The point is that the fundamental structure of the sites is entirely sound and relies on time-tested approaches.

If you're considering an extreme theme I urge you to carefully consider how it impacts usability. Sacrificing this for the sake of a theme is a mistake.

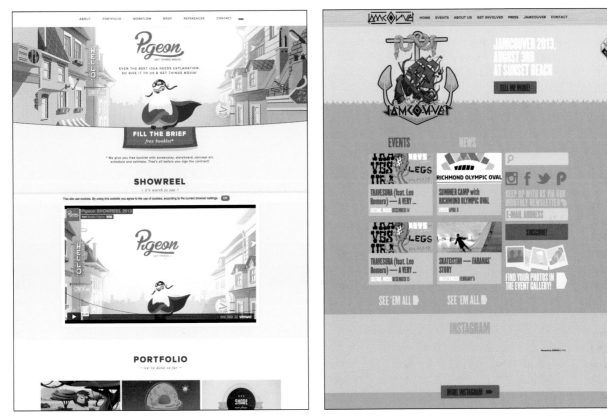

FIGURE 1: www.studiopigeon.com

FIGURE 3: www.jamcouver.com

FIGURE 2: www.pncchristmaspriceindex.com

FIGURE 4: www.une-cuisine-astucieuse.fr

www.loveless-shop.jp

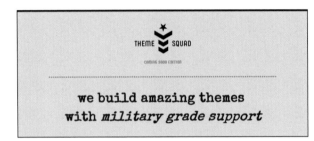

http://themesquad.com

www.trezee.com

www.exsus.com/highway-one-roadtrip

http://islreview.com

www.thetownthatcameinfromthecold.com

http://w-not.ru

www.impero-festive-meter.com

06/Futuristic

In this chapter I want to highlight a rather fringe thematic style: the futuristic landscape. At times it makes sense to create a futuristic theme, especially when the content is specifically futuristic. Such is the case with sites like the Smithsonian Channel's Rise of the Robots **(FIGURE 1)**. The theme makes perfect sense as the content is intended to be futuristic. In this case the theme is obvious and not surprising in the least.

This obvious connection works really well. On the opposite end of the spectrum, it can be really interesting when a theme runs counter to our presumptions. For example, the TV show *Firefly* features a futuristic version of cowboys. At first this strikes most people as ridiculous, but the show was a hit and has a huge cult following despite its short lifespan. The point is that unexpected juxtapositions can be powerful.

Though we can't find such extreme contrast in the examples I have provided here, the theme does have an interesting power that Firefly highlights. It can bring new life and a modern twist to just about anything. For example, finding premade designs is not all that hard. There are numerous websites where one can purchase countless designs for just about anything—all premade. The Infinity **(FIGURE 2)** product is essentially a set of premade design assets for the web. However, it has its own subtle twist that sets it apart—essentially it is more modular. In this case the futuristic space theme establishes the mentality that this is something new, that it is somehow different. It is an interesting way to leverage the theme to set one's site apart.

In other cases, the theme is simply used for fun or decoration. The Kojo site **(FIGURE 3)** is an example of pure decoration. In this case, the theme is rather subtle and one might argue that there is no theme at all. Contrast this with CoolApps **(FIGURE 4)** where the theme is simply fun. I don't get an industry-changing-vibe as much as I get that the folks behind the site are probably easygoing and fun to work with.

This particular approach is rather flexible. It might seem out of place at first, but a theme like this can transform a boring topic into a fun one.

FIGURE 1: www.smithsonianchannel.com/sc_assets/html/bionicman

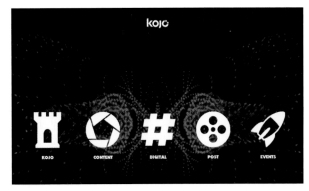

FIGURE 3: http://kojo.com.au

FIGURE 2: http://originalmockups.com/bundles/infinity-bundle

FIGURE 4: www.coolappse.com

www.srgint.com

http://blinkss.com

http://kari-na.com

http://mooncampapp.com

06/Holiday

Although it might seem at first that a section on holiday branding will be extremely limited in use, I disagree. In contrast, I think we can learn a lot from the holiday-themed examples provided here. It strikes me that some of the samples demonstrate what happens when designers get a little bit of room to work, when the reigns are loosened and they are allowed to more freely explore. Some of the samples are simply demonstrations of how a little holiday decoration can be added. In other cases, we find thematic skins on top of the normal design. Finally, many of the samples are actually niche microsites intended as marketing and promotional assets targeting the holidays. This is obviously a lot of ground to cover. As a result I have collected a few more samples here than I normally do. This is particularly useful given that many of these sites will be gone or changed after the holiday.

In the e-commerce world, it has become commonplace to apply simple holiday elements to a site. Sites like Bluefly **(FIGURE 1)**, REI **(FIGURE 2)** and Gifts.com **(FIGURE 3)** are but a few examples of this approach. In all of these, the site fundamentally remains unchanged. Holiday elements have simply been woven into the design. Some tweak the logo; others simply add a background image. I actually go back and forth on whether this matters at all to consumers. I fully understand that I am overly observant of these things and that I am perhaps overthinking things. That said, I really do wonder if consumers notice it—or care—at all. I am sure that if you applied such a theme in the middle of summer you would get some serious grief for it and it would certainly be noticed. Keep in mind that during the holidays we are bombarded with images of holly, Christmas trees, Santa Claus and so on. A usability study to dissect this would be really interesting.

In other cases, the entire purpose of the site is related to the holidays. Consider for example the Flying X-Mas Trees **(FIGURE 4)** and the Why You Love Christmas **(FIGURE 5)** websites. Both of these exist as promotional sites related to the holiday. I would be really eager to see statistics on these sites and how they help an agency. It seems that these are the modern day equivalent to a Christmas card to the world.

At the end of the day, these thematic sites are interesting to consider. And I really believe you can glean some interesting ideas from them, even if it happens to be the middle of the summer!

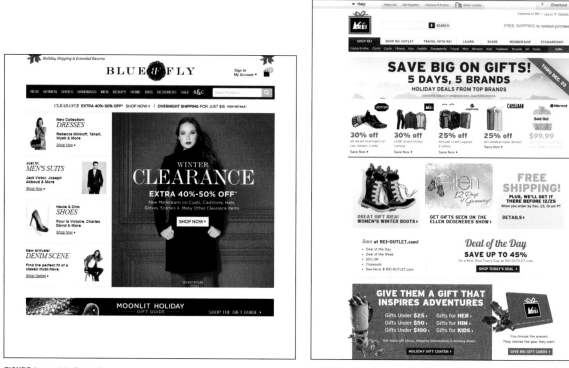

FIGURE 1: www.bluefly.com/

FIGURE 2: www.rei.com

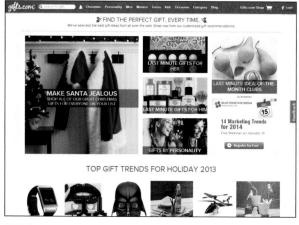

FIGURE 3: www.gifts.com

FIGURE 4: http://2014.studio38.ru

FIGURE 5: http://xmas.acc.cc

www.holidaysineverett.com

www.barnesandnoble.com

www.rakuten.com

http://tasarimgezegeni.com/2014/en

http://oldnavy.gap.com

www.landsend.com

www.wizfactorystudios.com

http://ainsworthelementary.org/hometour

http://www.cafepress.com/

www.sears.com

http://arketi.com/holiday2013/

07/

Navicons On the Desktop • Jumbo Animated Sidebars • Teaser Screen • Decorative Text • Atypical Navigation • Icons • Instant Sign-Up • Transparency • Ribbons • Prompt to Scroll • In-Page Navigation • Ornamental • Video Backgrounds • Geometric Shapes

DESIGN ELEMENTS

Design elements come in a wide array of shapes, sizes and styles. Some reflect purely trendy approaches, while others are the result of necessity. What is truly fascinating about these groupings is that each and every one of them has a purpose. Each of them has a way of being used that elevates it from randomness to a clear purpose. And yet, each of these elements can be wasted and reduced to a worthless role when used without intent. Even worse, when neglected, these design elements actually detract from the design they are a part of. The moral of the story is to not just blindly follow what others are doing. Perhaps you presume you need to use a navicon as part of your navigation. This might be true, but don't just assume so because it is what everyone is doing. Instead, step back and consider what makes the most sense. Sometimes the best solution isn't what everyone else is doing.

07/Navicons On the Desktop

One trend that is interesting to observe is how mobile web design is taking precedence over the desktop. In days gone by we designed for the desktop and maybe, if we were lucky, we would design a mobile alternative. With responsive design we started by taking our desktop sites and mashing them into smaller screens. Now the industry seems to be rapidly shifting toward a mobile-first mentality. In this world we design for the mobile web and then as an afterthought (a bit of an overstatement for drama's sake) we consider what it will look like on the desktop. This particular trend, the use of navicons on desktop sites, is a natural result of the influence of the mobile web.

Navicons started out as an element for mobile web designers to use. It was a convenient way to tuck a large amount of content (typically navigation) into a hidden element. One touch and out pops a large set of navigation. When you're dealing with tiny screens, you really have to get creative with how you use the space available to you. So in this chapter we look at situations where the navicon is not only on the mobile version, but also is in use on the desktop. It seems that designers have found it useful for stuffing navigation and other bits into hiding—and bringing it back out via a handy dandy navicon.

I will say that one thing about this annoys me, and it has little to do with the use of them on the desktop: I strongly encourage you to consider labeling your navicon. I know that adding the word "menu" next to it really clutters things up. But I have observed many times that users are still not aware of what a navicon is and does. Believe it or not, the rest of the world is not obsessed with the navigation patterns on the mobile web. The Younger website **(FIGURE 1)** does exactly this: they have the navicon with a label next to it. The icon itself is simply not well known enough to function entirely on its own. Naturally, we can easily find sites that don't do this, and ironically some of them work really well. The Nine site **(FIGURE 2)** is a great example. Here the navicon is not labeled. I can't help but notice, though, that the site is insanely simple, and there is not much else to click on, and as a result the navicon is not easily lost in the design.

FIGURE 1: www.theyounger.co.uk

www.bloomberg.com

FIGURE 2: www.nine.is

http://paywhatyouwant.eu

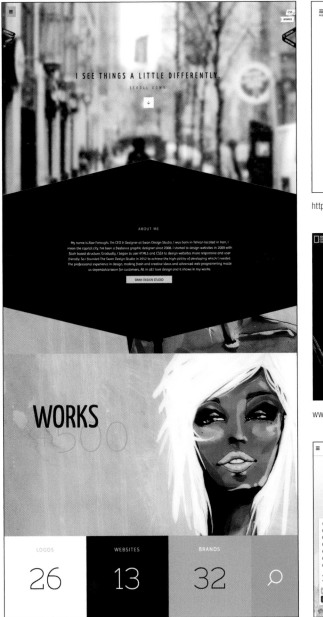

http://aleeforoughi.com

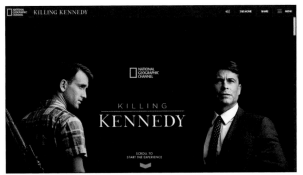

http://wandaprint.com/home

www.kennedyandoswald.com

http://mymail.my.com

http://adcade.com

http://litbloc.com

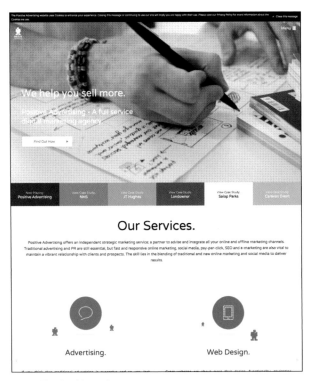

www.positiveadvertising.co.uk

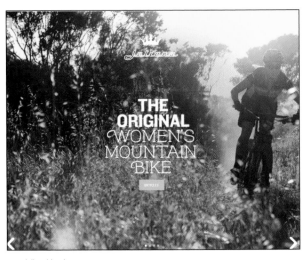

www.julianabicycles.com

07/Jumbo Animated Sidebars

Another trend that has found its way from the world of mobile web design into that of the desktop is the animated, jumbo-sized slide-out sidebar. Most often these elements contain an assortment of navigation elements, but as you can see in the examples it is not limited to a boring list of links. Instead, many designers take this opportunity to create a beautiful atypical navigation element that works really well.

What I find interesting about these is that they give the user access to the site's navigation at any time, but don't interfere with the content of the page. Some sites lend themselves to random browsing, but in other cases you want to direct users. This tool can be used to guide users based on the content of the page, but allow them access to navigation tools when they want to take control.

My favorite example among the sites collected here is the Dr. Woe website **(FIGURE 1)**. When closed, the sidebar provides access to a few key elements: audio controls, a link to home and a link to open the menu. I thought it was particularly clever to make a portion of the sidebar visible at all times and provide access to key elements. Click on the navicon and out slides a larger panel of tools. This includes the site's navigation, the owner's contact information and links to various social media. The navigation is kind of obvious and is what people typically put into these panels. However, the latter two elements are typically placed in the content of a page. Hiding them in the sidebar cleans up the design and presents an interesting way to simplify a page. This is the sort of discovery that compels me to keep writing my books. I am constantly amazed that designers continue to find innovative approaches to building webpages, and it is truly inspiring.

The 96 Elephants website **(FIGURE 2)** also uses this element in a creative way. The site actually makes use of two jumbo animated sidebars (though the screenshot only shows the one on the left). The right side contains the petition form for users to complete. I thought this was an interesting way to bring the actual desired action of the site directly to the user. When the page firsts loads the panel is revealed. Users can then hide it away and reopen it at any time. It is a clever way to get the user to see and acknowledge the action item of the site.

FIGURE 1: http://drwoe.nl

FIGURE 2: http://96elephants.org

www.evver.com

www.allesistgut.ru

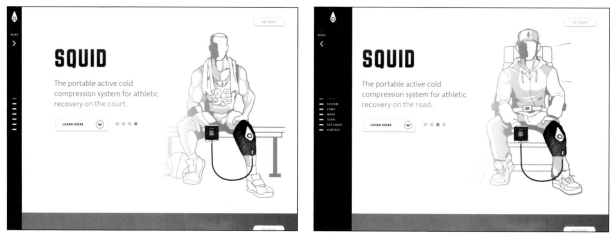

http://squidcompression.com

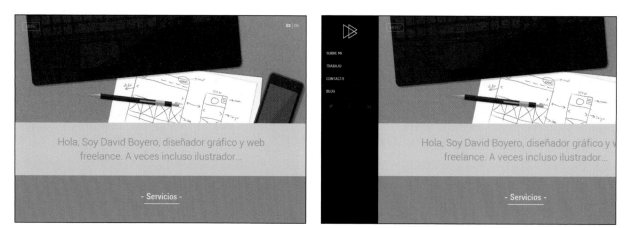

http://davidboyero.com

07/Teaser Screen

It isn't all that surprising to find that a trend rises from the past to find its way into the modern designer's tool belt. Such is the case with the teaser screen. At the height of the Macromedia Flash boom (2007ish) there were countless sites that used preloaders. These preloaders were often entertaining hooks that attempted to get you interested in the site while the remainder of the content (a flash movie as it were) loaded. We sometimes see a hint of this in modern web design. I have titled this section teaser screens instead of pre-loaders because they do not function as a waiting screen for something to load. Instead, they serve as a doormat that welcomes people to the site and entices them to dig further.

While I am a proponent of putting the content front and center and forgoing such an approach, the format does have some interesting potential. One thing that occurs to me is that you could use these as a way to get people interested enough to keep digging; just give them some tantalizing nugget that makes them want more. I can't help but wonder if the investment the user makes at this point will make them more likely to stay on the site and find out exactly what it is all about. It is an interesting theory anyway, but one that would require testing to verify or disclaim.

Another interesting aspect of this approach is the ability to set a stage for something—in particular, if you are competing in a crowded marketplace. In fact, if you look at the samples here, they are almost entirely from industries and niches that are extremely saturated. I think a real potential of this approach is to try to put a different twist, tone or spin on your product before people find out exactly what it is. By doing so, you attempt to genuinely look and feel different. Do you have yet another portfolio site in competition with thousands upon thousands of others? Perhaps an entryway teaser page with a compelling message is what you need.

Consider the Rainjar website **(FIGURE 1)**. This site represents a to-do list application. Certainly this is nothing new. In fact, it is perhaps one of the most redundant type of app ever. You could easily find hundreds of alternatives. And on a basic level, it is hard to imagine that any one of them is really more than checking items off. But I am not here to argue if the Rainjar app is better or unique: I am only proposing that their site and the layout they have chosen sets them apart. It is a vivid use of the approach in very intentional way.

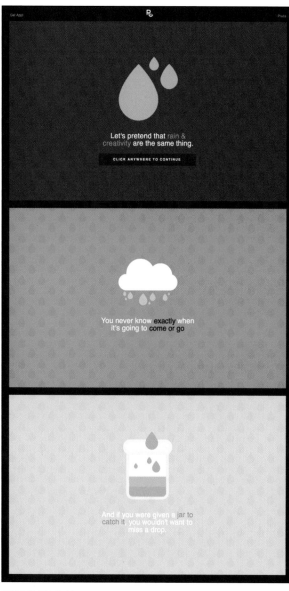

FIGURE 1: http://rainjar.co

http://reducing-the-obvious.de

www.vacheron-constantin.com/en/metiers-d-art-florilege

www.dearmum.org

http://makeyourmoneymatter.org

www.justrightforchildren.com

http://150px.com

www.mijlo.com/essentials

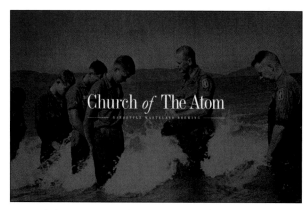

www.atomkyrkan.se

www.cultivatedwit.com

http://themeat.in

www.hioscar.com

07/Decorative Text

Most designers agree that text can be beautiful. In so many ways text and typography are the most critical element to any form of design. Text is a necessary component of design, and fortunately it is often something of beauty. In the samples I have collected here, the sites go beyond simply beautiful text. They have truly transformed elements of text into small works of art that are gorgeous and beautiful all on their own. Their ability to communicate while providing a level of decorating and beauty to the page only makes them that much more amazing. If you are interested in turning some text into a focal point or an almost illustrated element for your site, be sure to analyze the samples provided here. Let's look more closely at a few of the sites I have collected.

I love all of the sites in this chapter, but a few stand out. The Serve Seattle site **(FIGURE 1)** is one such site. Though the decorative text over the image appears to be hand rendered, it is actually a decorative typeface. When I was in design school I drove my teachers nuts because I was always finding ways to work in decorative typefaces such as this one. While designers often rely on a variety of classic typefaces, there is always room for the niche decorative typefaces. The trick, as with any design element, is to make sure it fits perfectly and that it serves to reinforce the message of the site. I fully admit that I have a bit of a bias toward this style; all the same, I think it is a legitimate pattern worth commenting on. I believe the Serve Seattle site executes this beautifully.

Another example here that I really love is The Pete Design site **(FIGURE 2)**. In this case, the design certainly uses decorative text to create an overall beautiful design. But here the typefaces used are not at all decorative. In contrast, they are relatively conservative typefaces. The beauty of the text is achieved through a delicate structure, color and decoration. The result is that the text not only decorates the page, but also serves as the primary communication point. This multifunctional solution is elegant and useful.

In some cases, such as the Fillet website **(FIGURE 3)**, the text transcends mere decoration and becomes small works of art. In this case the elements are less informational and more decorative. Scroll through this gem of a site and you get a feel for just how artistic type can be—it is genuinely inspiring.

FIGURE 1: http://serveseattle.org

FIGURE 2: www.thepetedesign.com

FIGURE 3: www.fillet.com.br

www.ridebarstow.com

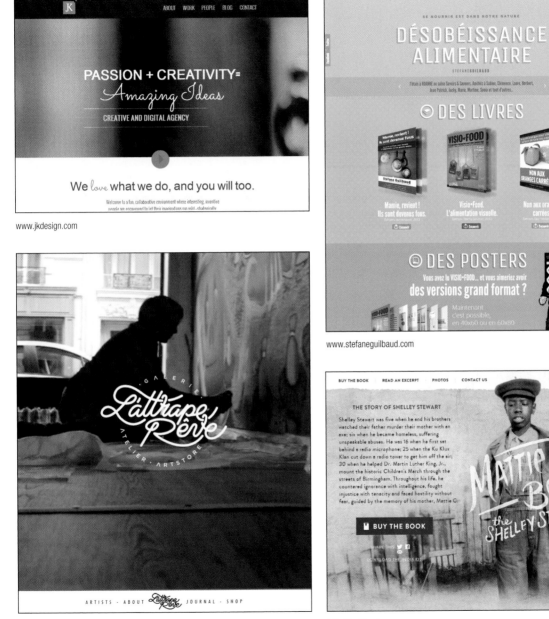

www.jkdesign.com

www.stefaneguilbaud.com

www.lattrapereve.fr

http://mattiecsboy.com

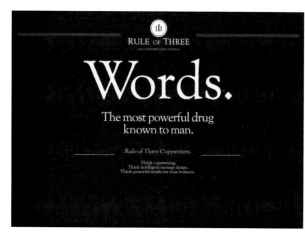

http://rule-of-three.co.uk

http://newmansfish.com

http://gutsandgloryand.us

www.knucklesindustries.com

07/Atypical Navigation

For as much as I encourage designers to follow common design patterns, I equally love and appreciate it when they throw them out the window. The sites collected here do just that; in particular they each put their own unique twist on site navigation. Trying out alternative approaches to navigation certainly seems like an endeavor with some serious risks involved. What if your navigation is not easily understood or does not match the mental model users have of your content? What if your creativity makes the site worse and even possibly entirely unusable? A lot of what-ifs, to be certain. Most of the time, I would highly recommend you not experiment with navigation—just rely on the tried and true models. The only way beyond this, in my humble opinion, is if you are willing to do user testing.

If you are willing and able to test your designs on actual users, you are welcome to try anything you want. In fact, if you are able to do so, you can try just about anything! User testing will either show it performs better or worse. Users will either accomplish the goals you give them or they won't. Shape your unique solution to fit the exact purpose of the site and you will naturally flow towards the best—and perhaps most elegant—solution. Frankly, this sums up the entire idea behind any user-centered design model. In such a world, norms and patterns are starting points to build on.

One of my favorites collected here is the Adidas career site **(FIGURE 1)**. On this site, the navigation begins anchored to the bottom of the screen. When you consider the flow of the site, it is remarkably smart. It might just seem like a clever idea that some designer is using to feel creative; I assure you there is much more to it. As you consume the content of the home page, the navigation logically follows the main content. You are not likely inspired to navigate around until you read a bit, so it makes tremendous sense that the navigation would be after the content. What really makes me happy, though, is that they moved the navigation to the top once you click through to a sub page. Amazingly it actually animates from bottom to top: this informs me of the change. Again, one might think this is trivial, but there is much more at work. Once I have clicked, the navigation takes on more importance—I am invested in navigating the site and it now makes perfect sense to be at the top. Typically, I would not be a fan of moving navigation, but here it fits the content and works brilliantly.

FIGURE 1: www.adidasretailjobs.com

www.protest.eu/en

www.lacoste.com/polo

www.theforestersmusic.com

THE MAN

TO EAT

SLIDERS

PIZZA

SHARE

TACOS

TO DRINK

http://thebotanist.com.au

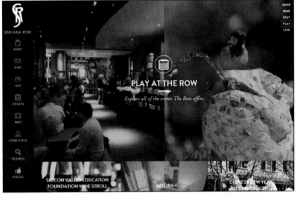

www.santanarow.com

www.citan.mercedes.fr

http://shopmack.com

www.fluttuo.com

http://remotejobs.io

www.digitalpod.co.uk

http://2013.unknowncroatia.com

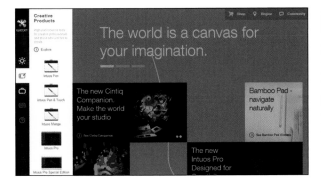

www.mcdonalds.co.uk/ukhome/promotions/favourites.html

www.wacom.com/en/us

http://50north5th.com

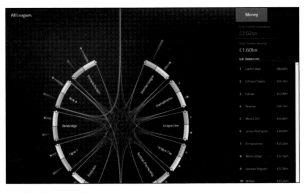

http://transferwindow.info

07/Icons

Icons have long been an element of graphic design. In fact, one might even consider them among the very oldest. Icons and pictograms have been at work since the very beginning of the written word. Some early languages were essentially built on them. It should come as no surprise to find them among modern web designs: They are incredibly useful design elements that both inform users and decorate a design. Naturally, some sites use them in more prominent ways than others.

Among the sites here, a few stand out. One such site is the Calester landing page **(FIGURE 1)**. Here the logos serve as landmarks to get you reading the content. They decorate the page and give it beauty, but they also direct your attention. It is really important to note the visual consistency of the icons they used; the fact that the icons go together perfectly due to a consistent design style cannot be overstated. Many people attempt designs like this one, but fail to unify the icons with a single style. The results always look half-baked and lame. This is perhaps the most vivid caution I would make with this style. If you cannot unify the icons, you should find an alternate design solution.

I really love the use of icons on the Greyp Bikes site **(FIGURE 2)**. Here the icons add a level of style and beauty to the page. But more then this, they reinforce the navigation. Though not all of the icons used are literal translations, they have made a tremendous effort to ensure that the icons mean something. Through the use of direct references to the elements of the bike they completely nail it. It might have been tempting to use a wrench for mechanical, for example, but that is detached from the bike. The custom icons they made for this design really bring it to life and give it a vividly unique style.

I like to show my web design students the mediaBOOM site **(FIGURE 3)**. The animated icons bring the site to life in a fun and engaging way when you hover over them. The icons encourage you to click and explore the contents of the site. They are beautiful and blend into the design, but they also hook the user in a unique and creative way. I also can't help but nerd out over the fact that they made them with scalable vector graphics.

FIGURE 1: http://calester.com

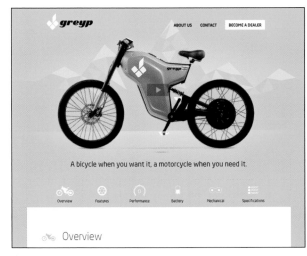

FIGURE 2: www.greyp-bikes.com

FIGURE 3: http://mediaboom.com

http://smashingconf.com/ny-2014

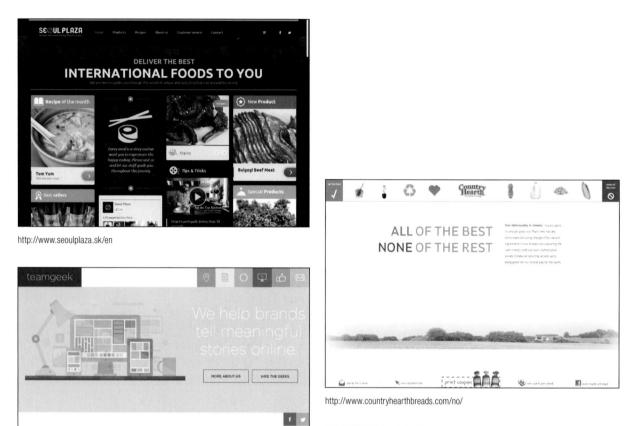

http://www.seoulplaza.sk/en

www.teamgeek.co.za

http://www.countryhearthbreads.com/no/

www.vvicrew.com

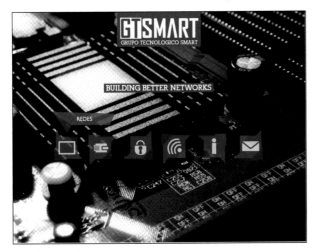

www.yribarren.com/gtsmart

http://pinpointsocial.com

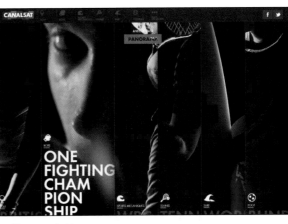

http://sports.canalsat.fr

www.trask-industries.com

07/Instant Sign-Up

Though I don't really think this is a new trend, it is the first time I have identified the pattern and talked about it. This chapter features sites that offer some sort of service that you must register for. Instead of using a call-to-action button that takes users to a registration form, these sites place the form right on the landing page. Obviously this approach works particularly well when your registration process is extremely simple.

The approach makes good sense to me. If your sign-up form includes only 1–3 fields, why bother asking people to click a button to get there? By showing them just how simple the form is, you might just entice people to sign up. I think it is a really interesting idea worth exploring. If you do want to try this, I strongly recommend that you test the idea using some form of A/B testing. This will be the only real way to find out if the approach works best for you.

The biggest contradiction that I can see with this format is that asking someone to sign up when they only just got there is a little premature—even too direct. Imagine that you meet someone and instead of striking up a conversation, you just immediately ask him or her out on a date. It would likely come off as awkward and probably a little creepy. Depending on your product or service, putting the sign-up form front and center might come off this way. At the end of the day, it is an interesting idea that challenges our presumptions about what goes where—that is the exact point of this book. Hopefully this sparks some ideas that make you reconsider the presumptions you might have about your site's structure.

In my opinion, it is an approach that lends itself well to casual services like Penflip **(FIGURE 1)**. Though a service like this might become critical to your workflow, it starts off as just a casual tool. That is to say, you sign up and play around with it. It isn't a big deal.

For much more serious or significant services, such as Mint **(FIGURE 2)**, it seems like asking users to sign up straight away is a bit awkward. This service, after all, hooks into your bank account and is not something to do on a whim. But the more I consider the site, the more sense it makes. After all, it sounds complicated to set such a thing up. But look at that: I can sign up without giving them anything beyond my email address. In that way, they ease you into the service, instead of asking for a mountain of personal information up front.

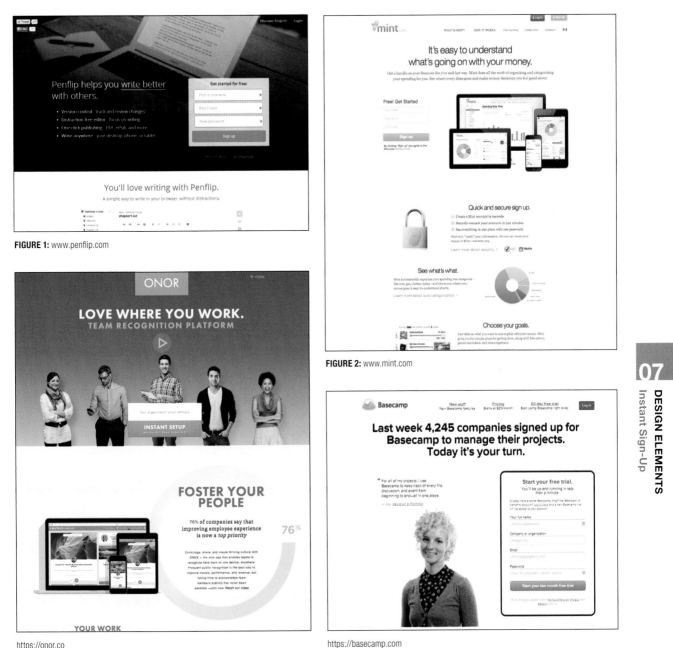

FIGURE 1: www.penflip.com

FIGURE 2: www.mint.com

https://onor.co

https://basecamp.com

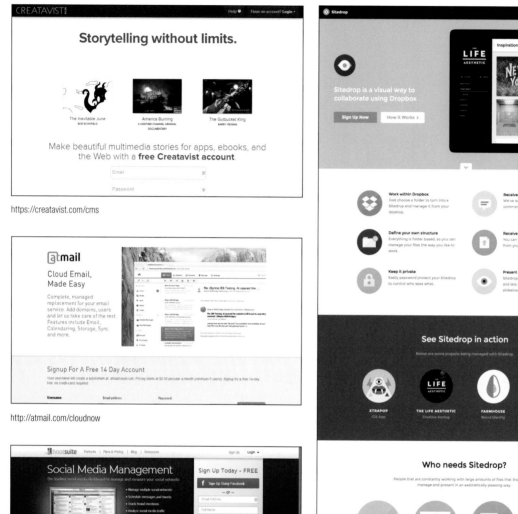

https://creatavist.com/cms

http://atmail.com/cloudnow

https://hootsuite.com

http://sitedrop.com

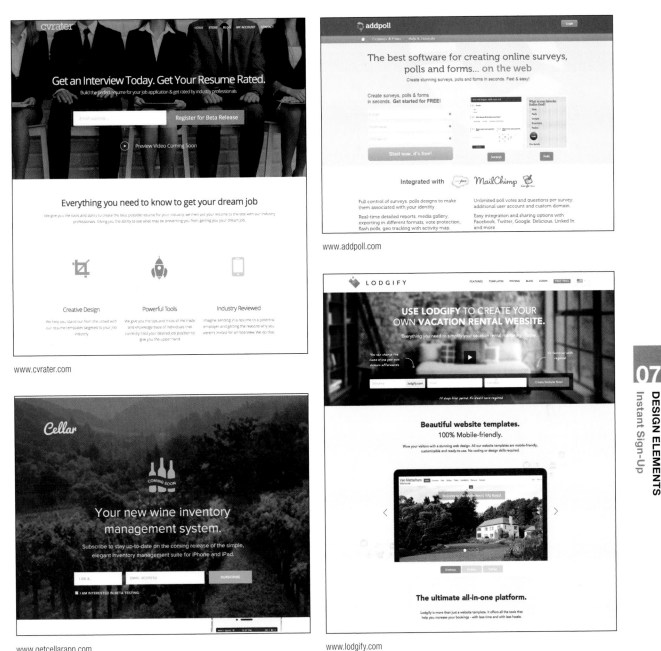

www.cvrater.com

www.addpoll.com

www.getcellarapp.com

www.lodgify.com

07/Transparency

As I have often said, some patterns are exciting and interesting. Transparency is anything but exciting. Though it might lack in the excitement category, it is a useful option that is used surprisingly infrequently. In fact, the items collected here were not all that easy to find and took a considerable amount of hunting to put together. Although there is nothing special about the approach, it seems to come and go as a popular element. Right now it is actually not all that popular. This is exactly why I find it inspiring and include it here.

I noticed a few home page forms that made use of the effect on the text entry boxes. SEM Compass **(FIGURE 1)** and Rist Job **(FIGURE 2)** take slightly different approaches but both have worked transaprency into their forms. This is a subtle and decorative touch that doesn't make or break a design. What I do appreciate is how it unifies the composition and makes the form a part of the page, not just something stacked on top of it.

It seems that the creation of space and depth is another natural use with this technique. For example, Tony Chester's site **(FIGURE 3)** has a container around the content with a transparent background. This container, as you can see, is layered between his photo and the background. Overall it gives the illusion of depth, which is greatly reinforced by the transparency.

In a few situations, transparency is actually used in rather conceptual and meaningful ways. The best example I found was the Circle website **(FIGURE 4)**. The site is about finding what's happening near you. The transparent card the hand is holding up shows content as though it is a display of some type. The transparency allows the real world to show through it and onto the device. I get the impression that they want you to think of it bringing the real world in. Through transparency, they connect an imaginary interface with the cityscape. It is an interesting and thoughtful approach.

In many other cases the element is really just a form of decoration. This is the most likely explanation for the usage in at least half of the examples provided here. But don't take that as a ding on the style. I think it is a really useful and subtle tool, especially considering how easy it is to implement real transparency in code and with PNGs these days.

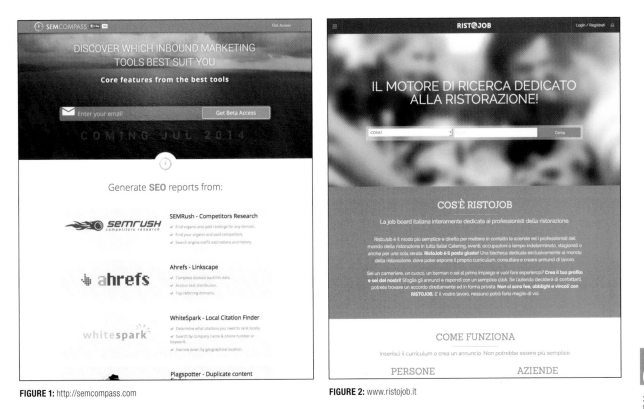

FIGURE 1: http://semcompass.com

FIGURE 2: www.ristojob.it

FIGURE 3: http://tonychester.com

FIGURE 4: http://circleapp.com

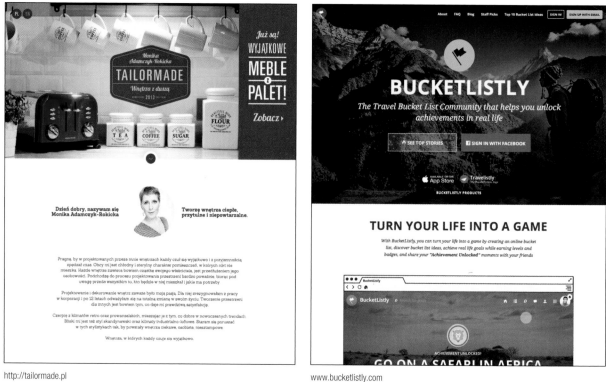

http://tailormade.pl

www.bucketlistly.com

www.musicaddictdesigner.com

www.avalancheranch.com

http://www.mehdi-benyounes.cwom/fr/lead-developpeur-webdesigner-chef-de-projet/index.html

www.thehippohouse.com

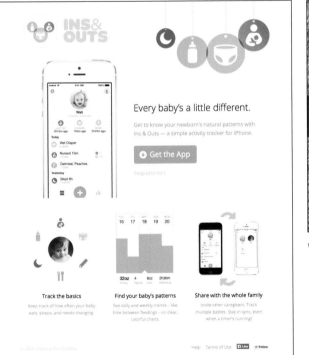

http://insandoutsapp.com

www.suavia.it

07/Ribbons

In Volume 3 of my Idea Books, I featured a section on ribbons and frankly I thought it was a style that had run its course. At the time of that book's writing, the use of fabric textures and fancy edge treatments were both particularly popular. This combination worked well and was a defining visual of the time period. As I said, I thought the trend was over. But this is not the case: it turns out that ribbons are still rather popular, but with a new twist. Instead of attempting to create more realistic ribbons with fabric textures, designers have merged the element with the ever-popular flat design style.

A perfect demonstration of this is the Festival Guide **(FIGURE 1)**. Here the flat style is at work (though the ribbon does have a fairly unrealistic drop shadow that sets it apart from the background). Note that it doesn't attempt to look photorealistic, and the basic shadow works well in this design. The most interesting twist here is that the ribbon element is actually the main call to action. Though it doesn't look like a button, we understand what it does based on the action-oriented text and the placement on the page. It somehow feels like the thing a user should go do. I am always impressed with something feels natural and intuitive; I tend to think it is an elegant solution when this magic combination happens.

In other cases like the Timmy Tompkins site **(FIGURE 2)** or Alkopedia **(FIGURE 3)** and even James Hsu **(FIGURE 4)**, the ribbons are more or less used as decorative elements. In some ways, they serve to attract attention to what you might consider the beginning of the content. In this way they help drive the user's focus. But I would only give this element a trivial amount of credit for this in these designs. In reality, there is nothing wrong with using something just because it is beautiful. It might not be as graceful or minimalist, but who cares? As you can see here, the results are beautiful and fit the modern web nicely. The ribbons work perfectly.

One of the more unique uses of the element that I have seen can be found on the Super Sync website **(FIGURE 5)**. This experimental site from Google has an extremely distinct style and its illustration-based design feels unique. It is not surprising that Google would innovate, but I am surprised at the creative focus of this site. The story the site tells and the experience you have discovering it is amazing. The ribbon here simply serves as a supporting element in the overall content—there is no deep meaning that gives the element purpose. It is just yummy.

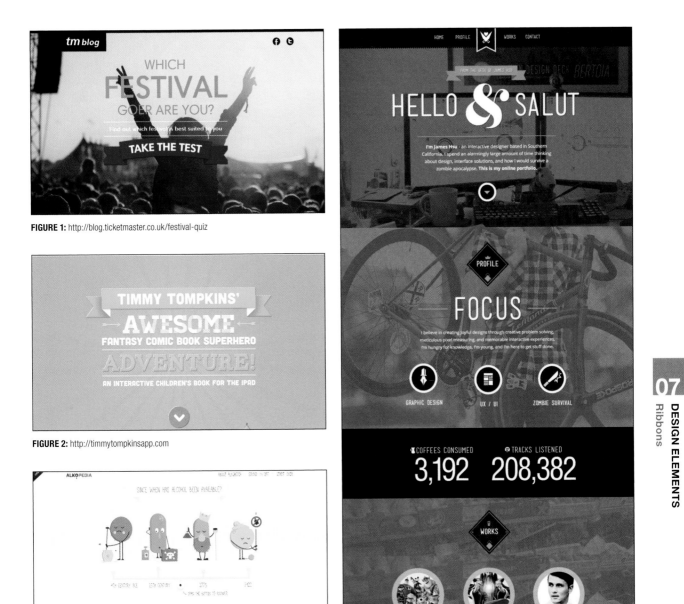

FIGURE 1: http://blog.ticketmaster.co.uk/festival-quiz

FIGURE 2: http://timmytompkinsapp.com

FIGURE 3: http://alkopedia.dareville.com

FIGURE 4: www.hellojameshsu.com

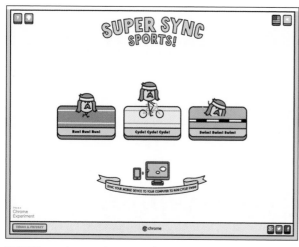

FIGURE 5: www.chrome.com/supersyncsports

www.pedalingnowhere.com

www.mrvisual.info

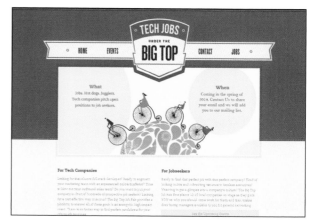

http://bigtop.it

www.aprijic.com

www.the53rdparallel.com

www.ejectorseat.co.uk

http://teslathemes.com

07/Prompt to Scroll

Like transparency, another somewhat mundane element is the prompt to scroll. Elements like this tend to be more subtle elements that come define a slice of time in the web design world. For example, snap back to the web 2.0 craze, complete with shiny designs. One such detail at that time was the badge. I featured this in Volume 1 of my books. It was a trivial element that was a hallmark of the time. Such is the case with the element presented in this chapter. Here I showcase a variety of sites that, upon landing on them, entice you to scroll down with some sort of element. There is a wide variety in terms of the content on the home page: some are void of content, others are packed with it. But all of them share an idea—to encourage users to scroll.

On the surface, this seems almost silly. After all, don't users know to scroll? It isn't as though scrolling is a new thing. On the contrary, I think it is interesting to have such an element. Every time I see one of these, I think of a little bell sitting on the counter of a store near the register, with a sign that says "Ring for service." Most people know what the bell is for even without the sign. So why label it? I think it is a sort of invitation, a verification of its purpose. Having an invitation to scroll suggests to users that the content below has a purpose.

On the web, a common pattern is to pack the most important content at the top of the page, and as you move down the page the content becomes less and less critical. This is not too much different from how news articles are written. Perhaps your site makes the most sense if you consume all the content. Or perhaps you simply have incredibly meaningful content below the fold. If so, entice your users to scroll with a simple invitation.

On many sites, this invitation is nothing more than a downward pointing arrow. Sites like the Oakley store **(FIGURE 1)** demonstrate this approach. It is a method that works, but frankly I think it can be improved upon. I tend to gravitate towards the Diesel **(FIGURE 2)** approach that not only points down, but also includes the word scroll. In this case, it is vividly clear what the user is supposed to do.

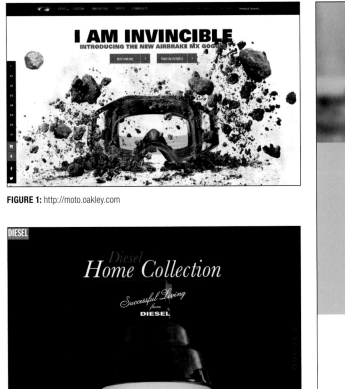

FIGURE 1: http://moto.oakley.com

FIGURE 2: www.diesel.com/collection-diesel-home

http://hthworldwide.net

www.obabyapp.com

http://lookbook.bolia.com

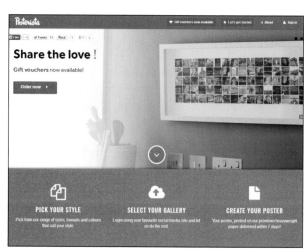

www.posterista.co.uk

www.mgo.com/dinner

www.phytech.com

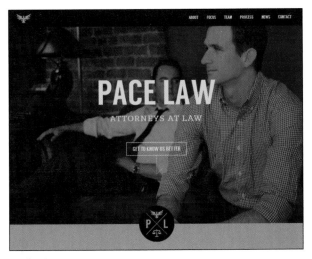

http://pacelaw.com

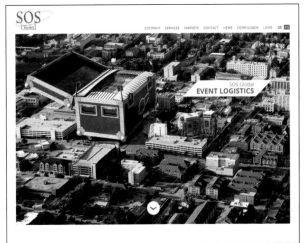

www.sosglobal.eu/en

www.paperandpaint.dk

www.mahedineyahia.fr

http://www.urbotip.com/

http://aynibrigade.com/

http://www.librotecaelgatodecheshire.es/

http://go.angrybirds.com/

07/In-Page Navigation

An extremely popular approach to designing pages is the single page site. In this model, an entire multipage website is packed into a single page. This might be an entire site, or it might be an entire section. For example, many product pages on major manufacturer's websites are really huge, singular pages used as a modern day brochure to sell the product. Inside of these pages there is a need for navigation. Even though it is a single page, quite often there are multiple blocks of content that can be treated as separate pages. Two common approaches have emerged as solutions to this need. The first is to have a navigation bar across the top that sticks to the top of the page as you scroll. The second is to place some sort of vertical navigation bar along the side of the site. This second approach is what I want to focus on here.

The main reason I have singled out this approach is that it tends to be less typical. The web has long relied on horizontal navigation systems at the top of sites. Therefore, I find this trend more interesting and inspiring to analyze as a potential solution.

I believe that the first version of this trend emerged as an adaptation of the typical content slider. More specifically, many sites rely on a series of dots where each represents a portion of the content. Clicking these dots scrolls you to that part of the page. This is an extremely popular approach and many of the examples here rely on this method. While the solution works, I have a few thoughts on it. First and foremost, I have a real concern about the lack of labels. Mystery navigation like this means the user has no clue what they are clicking on. And if they find something they like how do they find it again? Users would have to randomly click until they find it again. The usability of these sites would be enhanced with some sort of labeling system.

This naturally brings us to the second subset of sites found in this chapter. These sites also rely on the sidebar navigation approach. In contrast, they provide additional information about each block of content. From icons to text labels, the exact solutions vary, but the result is a much more clear navigation system. You can more easily find your way around, focusing on the content you care about most. And, as described above, you can find your way back to content you previously discovered. In my opinion, this is a much stronger use of the technique. Naturally, it takes more work to build, but I think the results are well worth the effort.

www.designeat.com

www.altek.com.tw/cubic

www.kitchenaid.com.br

http://lookbook.bolia.com/

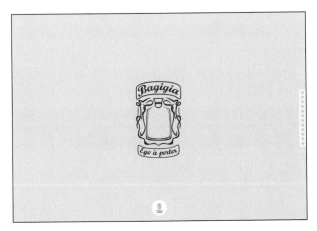

www.bagigia.com

http://fixedagency.com

http://unabridgedsoftware.com

www.parrot.com/flowerpower/en

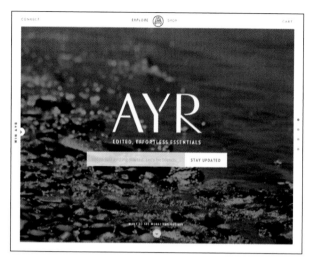

http://ayr.com

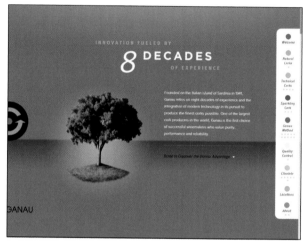

http://ganau.com

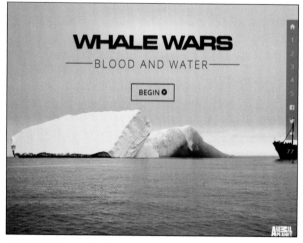

http://blood-and-water.animalplanet.com

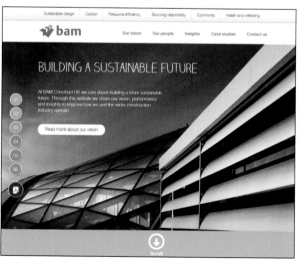

http://sustainability.bam.co.uk

07/Ornamental

Ornamental elements in web design are something I have observed and talked about since my first book, all the way back in 2008. And though designers have long relied on decorative elements, the use of ornament in web design has significantly changed over the years. If I had to sum up the change, I would suggest that the modern usage of the element is more subdued. It is part of the overall design, but not the main point. It supports and reinforces the brand, but the designs are not fundamentally set up to be ornate. Let's dissect a few examples to see how this might work.

Merchants On Long **(FIGURE 1)**, Healing Histories **(FIGURE 2)** and The Fudge House **(FIGURE 3)** are all perfect examples. In each of these (and even a few other samples here) the ornate elements are prominent and highly visible. However, they are not the focus. They accent the design. They help drive the user's attention. For example, the ornate framing of the logo on The Fudge House website gives it a more prominent place in the hierarchy of the design. In all of these, the use of ornament gives the design a specific style that sets the tone for the brand.

Please don't misinterpret my commentary on this style. I actually find it to be rather gorgeous and extremely effective. I would even argue that it is perhaps one of the oldest and most proven forms of decoration. I consider this to be among the most timeless of approaches. Consider that minimalism is a product of the twentieth-century; in contrast ornate design elements go back thousands of years. We find ornament in countless forms in the world's long history of art. This certainly seems like an element worth having in your toolbox.

In some of the examples here we find what might be considered more extensive usage of the style. The Ready to Inspire **(FIGURE 4)** website is a perfect example. Here the ornate style becomes a sort of theme. I could easily tag this as a nineteenth-century-style design, but in reality it is just built on a foundation of ornament.

Finally, you will find that many sites still simply use ornaments as repeating background patterns. Again, this is a tried and true approach that can be really beautiful. Ensuring that the pattern flows well with the foreground of the site is the most important thing to consider. This unification is critical in the success of the design. Then again, this is the case with *any* background element or pattern.

FIGURE 1: www.merchantsonlong.com

FIGURE 2: www.healinghistories.org

FIGURE 3: http://fudgehouse.co.uk

FIGURE 4: http://2014.inspireconf.com

http://jrichardhill.com

www.lulamag.com

www.villagrazioli.com

http://alicia-aubry.com

www.giardinopollensa.com

www.lizsbooksnuggery.com

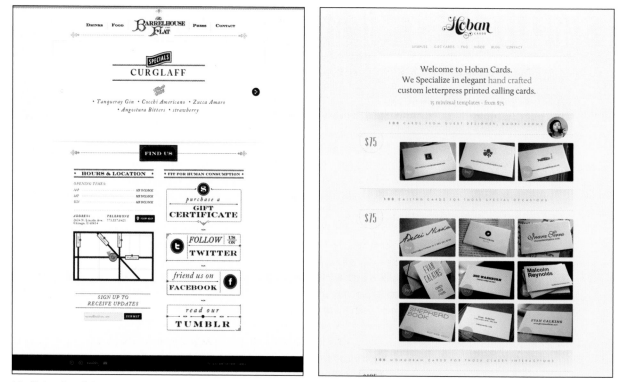

http://thebarrelhouseflat.com

https://hobancards.com

07/Video Backgrounds

A really interesting pattern that has been growing for some time now is the use of video as a background element. This approach has been around for quite some time. I can recall it being a common element of many all-Flash sites around 2008. With the implosion of Flash, web designers and developers let this one go. But as the web has progressed and we have slowly moved away from the traditional page format, this element has once again become popular.

There are two other factors that also contribute to the rise of this approach. First is the fact that high-speed Internet has become almost universal. I know not everyone has it, but stats show that as many as 72 percent of U.S. households have high speed Internet[1]. As such, large background videos (and the large file sizes they demand) are not as impractical as they once were. Secondly, there are several jQuery plug-ins that make adding large background videos to a site relatively easy. Video on the whole has become a much more prominent aspect of web design. In my opinion, this is a trend that will continue to take hold and only become more prominent with time.

This style could be used simply as decoration, which it sometimes is. You will find this true of several of the examples here. Personally though, I find it much more interesting when the technique is used for a greater purpose. Video has the potential to tell a story that reinforces the brand's purpose.

A fantastic example of this is the Spotify landing page **(FIGURE 1)** that uses a large background video. The message here is rather simple, and we can fully understand it even from this static image. The detail you are missing is that the video shows people in many settings listening to music. As a result, we get the idea that they provide music for every moment of life. This is an important message for the company. They are a digital music service, and most people probably presume it works best from a computer or perhaps an iPad. My instinct would be to not associate it with anything on the go. And yet, this is what almost all of the scenarios show: users on the go. I have no doubt this is intentional.

Don't use this style flippantly. Instead, carefully consider what it can do for you. If you just need some decoration for your site, there are much simpler ways to get there. And of course, to fully appreciate the samples here you really must visit the real sites!

1 http://www.ntia.doc.gov/blog/2013/household-broadband-adoption-climbs-724-percent

FIGURE 1: www.spotify.com/uk/video-splash

http://whenwasthelasttimeyoudidsomethingforthefirsttime.eastpak.com

http://ony.ru

http://couleecreative.com

http://riskeverything.us

www.whiteroomuk.com

www.lattrapereve.fr

http://whiteboard.is

http://telly.com/about

www.dadaabstories.org

www.nike.com/us/en_us/c/jordan/nike-jordan

www.lifeofpimovie.com

07/Geometric Shapes

For several chapters in this book, once I identified a topic, it took but a few minutes to find plenty of examples. Geometric patterns and shapes in web design is exactly such a topic. Obviously, if you can quickly identify a huge number of sites using a technique, it is a rather popular trend. There are two ways to approach this. You might consider this a sign that this is a good method. After all, it is very popular, and your site will feel at home among these other sites. This is perfect for brands that really need to look modern in order to break consumer assumptions. The second possibility is that this is an overused technique that should be taken out to pasture and is therefore to be avoided.

Perhaps it is obvious, but neither response is correct. In reality, this style, much like any other style we might latch onto, is just another tool in our arsenal. I would never suggest you build your personal style on a single trend like this. Instead, learn to work it to your benefit.

I really love this style. It has sort of become a minimalist version of ornamental design. The geometric shapes and patterns are often used as decorative flourishes, background elements and as containers for content in various ways. The results can be remarkably beautiful. I love how geometric shapes can give sites such beauty and style without becoming too much of a focal point.

Consider the personal site of Nate Navasca **(FIGURE 1)**. Here the pattern is extremely prominent. It serves as an eye-catching element that sets the site apart. Without this pattern the site would be yet another minimal site with solid colors. Instead, the pattern gives the site a distinct flavor. The best twist is this: the ornate background doesn't distract users from the main point of the site: the content. I am really intrigued by the way this element can be so prominent and yet not distracting. In fact, this strange correlation is something we find over and over again in the samples here.

For example, take a look at Perspective **(FIGURE 2)**, NEO **(FIGURE 3)** and Passeig de Gràcia **(FIGURE 4)**. All three of these rely on geometric patterns that are extremely prominent in the design. You just can't miss it. And yet, they don't keep us from the content for even a second. It seems to me that there are few ways to decorate a site without creating distractions. Perhaps this is why designers have fallen in love with it. It works so well as a supporting element.

FIGURE 1: http://navasca.com/nate

FIGURE 2: http://perspectivewoodworks.com

FIGURE 3: http://neolab.no

FIGURE 4: www.paseodegracia.com/en

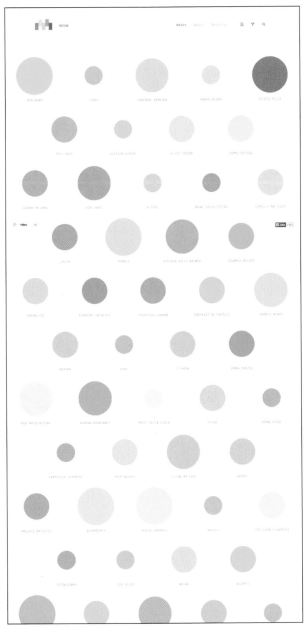

www.mosne.it

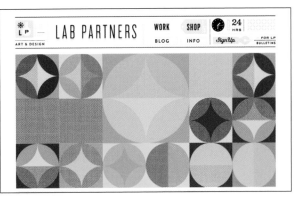

www.lp-sf.com

www.bellecour.fr

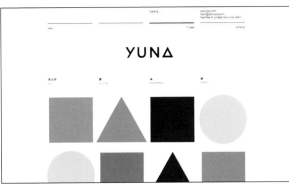

www.iamyuna.com

http://builtbybuffalo.com

www.hihayk.com

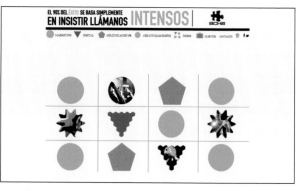

www.case-3d.com

www.acheproducciones.com

http://hellohikimori.com

http://webey.eu

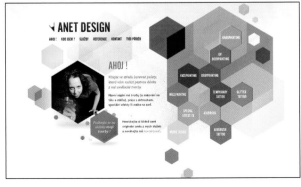

www.anet-design.cz

www.elrecibidor.com/es/home

08/

Responsive Images • Responsive Galleries • Responsive Navigation • Responsive Select Menus • Responsive Checkouts • Responsive Logins • Responsive Priorities • Responsive Bands of Content • Responsive Reformatting Layouts

RESPONSIVE ELEMENTS

It is hard to describe responsive design as a trend. Trends, after all, come and go. Though I have no doubt our approach to building websites will in time change, I am reasonably certain responsive design is here to stay for the foreseeable future. For those who are not yet aware of this approach, it is actually really simple to explain. Basically a responsive site adapts and changes the layout based on the screen size. For example, a site might have two columns of elements on the desktop version and then condense down to a single column for mobile devices. The content remains the same (for the most part), but the way the content is formatted changes.

One of the main reasons I started collecting sites by various categories (be it a trend, a style or a structure) was rather simple: I was intrigued by how various people solved the same problem. Though I seldom talk about it, this is perhaps the true purpose of my books: to see how others solve the same problem; to see how others use the same trend; to compare how others implement the same style and so on. Through this process of comparison, we inevitably find nuggets we love. Even better, we often piece together our own solutions that perfectly fit the problem at hand.

08/Responsive Images

Planning images for responsive layouts is a headache. It's hard enough to get good photos from clients. Getting them to work well in multiple layouts and formats is even harder. But as you will see in this section, a little creativity can result in some interesting solutions.

Those addressing responsive images seem to take one of three approaches. First, there is the "do nothing" camp, where the images simply scale up and down. Second, we have sites that replace all the images with different ones optimized to the layout at hand. Finally, there are sites that have a sort of sliding crop effect—where the crop of the photo changes as the size of the page changes. It is easy to understand why many people rely on the first approach; doing nothing is just much easier. The second two are more complex, but can result in images more suited to a device.

It's common sense that smaller screens need images with less detail, while larger screens, with more pixels to work with, can accommodate larger images containing more information. It is also common to find that desktop sites use taller images, while many mobile sites rely on horizontal images. A perfect demonstration of this is the Caddis website **(FIGURE 1)**. On the desktop version of this site, the images are in fact vertical. On the mobile version, they are displayed as horizontal. If you slowly resize your browser, you can watch how the images are simply cropped in a fluid way so as to fit the screen size. The technique here is hinged on the primary meat of the photo being placed inside a safe zone to the top left region of the photo.

The Lincoln Now **(FIGURE 2)** and Curadmír **(FIGURE 3)** sites are also excellent examples of what I would call responsive cropping. As you have no doubt realized, things get complicated fast and careful planning is key. With responsive design we must reconsider every single element of a website as we adapt it to each screen size.

One site that caught my eye for this category was the Somewhat site **(FIGURE 4)**, in particular their case study pages. On this site you will find a seldom-used fourth solution to this problem. Instead of adapting the image, they just make it go away. On the sample provided, they are showcasing a mobile app they built and the large background photo plays a supportive role. Rather than scaling or otherwise changing it, they simply remove it from the mobile design. At first this seems like a cop-out, but I think there is more to this approach than we might think.

FIGURE 1: www.caddis.co

FIGURE 2: http://now.lincoln.com

FIGURE 3: www.curadmir.com/home

FIGURE 4: www.somewhat.cc/case-study/lsn-global-app

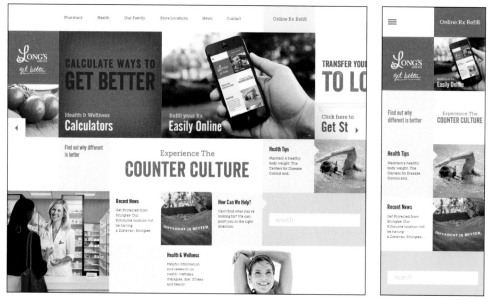

http://longsrx.com

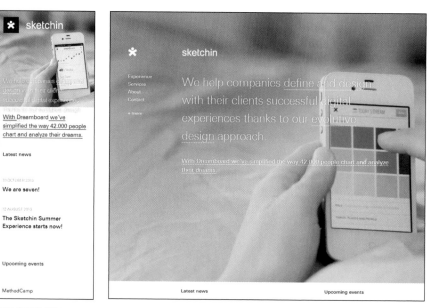

www.sketchin.ch/en

08/Responsive Galleries

If you thought dealing with single images in a responsive way is complicated, wait until you have to deal with a photo gallery. Things just get even more painful. It seems that the most common solution here is to simply scale things up and down to fit the screen. The secondary part of this is that the layouts change and reformat as the screen changes size. At smaller sizes, things tend to move toward a single column of photos while at larger screens they might have a mix of formats.

I Love Dust **(FIGURE 1)** demonstrates this approach perfectly. The desktop version highlights a single image by making it large, and below is a grid of other images. As you can see, the aspect ratio of the images means that on mobile devices, the first image is dominant. This is somewhat inconsequential to this site, but it is something that should be considered—in many cases, the images will have specific priorities that need to be respected. In this case, a great deal of flexibility means the site is probably a bit easier to maintain. Simply scaling image sizes will always be the easiest approach.

Another example that stuck out to me was the RSQ site **(FIGURE 2).** I am intrigued that on the desktop and tablet versions of this site, the logos on each portfolio piece are simple white silhouettes. But once it snaps to the mobile version, the logos get a semi transparent blue circle around them. Clearly the logos pop out better with this extra element. I contemplated this design for a long time to figure this out: My best guess is that by making the logos more visible the user might navigate the list more rapidly. This makes me wonder, if the circles make navigation on a mobile device easier, why not keep them on the desktop? After all, don't we want navigation there to be as easy as possible as well? Another thing to notice is that the images have a sliding crop effect. In this case, the meat of the image is in the middle. Once again, careful planning saves the day and ensures a maintainable site. Whatever the reasons behind this design, it is good for us to consider the results and how they might apply to our own work.

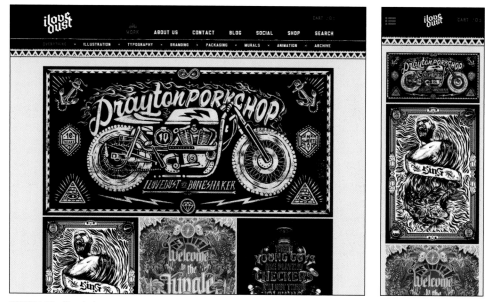

FIGURE 1: http://ilovedust.com

FIGURE 2: http://rsq.com/work/projects

http://rodmclean.com

www.erikford.me

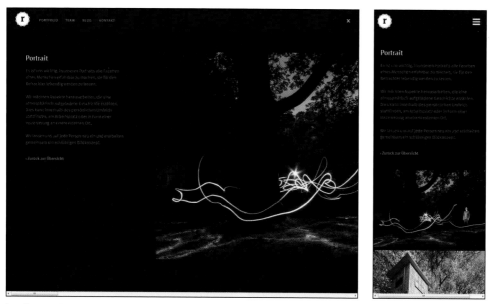

http://regentaucher.com/portfolio/portraits

http://mamochotena.pl

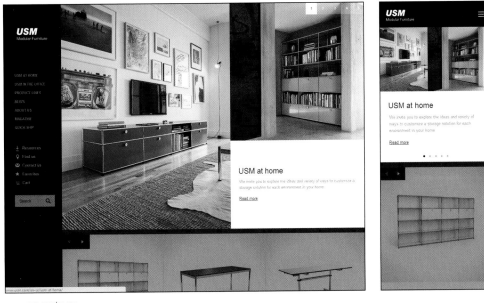

www.usm.com/en-us

www.emmytwenty.com

08/Responsive Navigation

Second to the actual content of a web page, I can't imagine a more critical element than navigation. The Internet is, of course, a web of pages interconnected. And navigation serves as the most prominent and important method of linking pages together. As with all other elements, responsive design has made designing site navigation a huge challenge. In fact, this is probably the one that demonstrates the most radical changes. Early on, designers just scaled the navigation. But this often meant that the first view of every page on a mobile device was a giant list of links for the navigation, and *not* the content. This had to change. As a result, we have seen a greater variety of solutions to this single problem than almost any other aspect of responsive design. Scan the samples here and you will notice a large range of methods at work. Let's dissect a few and see what is happening.

The Herschel Supply Co. site **(FIGURE 1)** demonstrates the most common approach. Here, the site has a relatively simple navigation system with just four items (plus the logo link to the home page). On mobile devices, they changed the horizontal list of links to a vertical one and hid it behind a navicon.

Other sites, such as Football as Football **(FIGURE 2)**, have far more complex navigation to wrangle into place. In this case, a massive menu is hidden behind a navicon on both desktop and mobile devices. It is based on four columns of links (as seen on the desktop version) and it condenses to a single column for mobile screens. Interestingly, the approach is useful in making both versions easier to navigate. It allows the content to be the primary focus, but gives the user access to navigation when they need it.

Another interesting approach can be found on the World Wildlife Fund site **(FIGURE 3)**. Here the desktop site has three levels of navigation in the main header: a main menu, a secondary menu and a set of call-to-action items. As the screen shrinks, they opted to hide most of the navigation behind a navicon while keeping the call-to-action items visible at all times. I appreciate that this demonstrates flexibility in any solution. They have adapted the method to perfectly fit their needs.

Finally, I want to focus your attention on *The Japan Times* website **(FIGURE 4)**. Once again, the site relies on an extremely complex navigation system that provides access to a wide range of content. As you can see in the mobile interface, they have translated the drop-down navigation system into a single column of links.

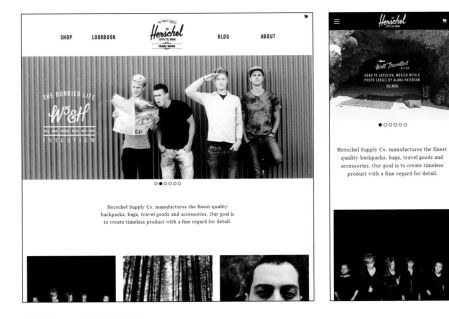

FIGURE 1: www.herschelsupply.com

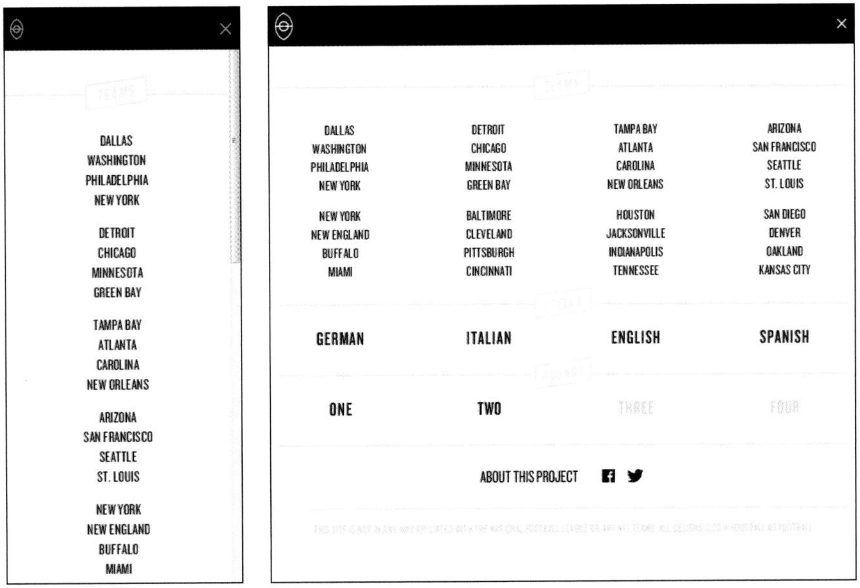

FIGURE 2: www.footballasfootball.com

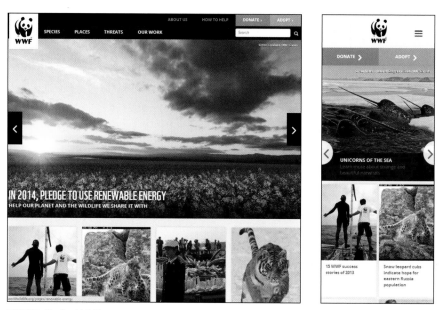

FIGURE 3: http://worldwildlife.org

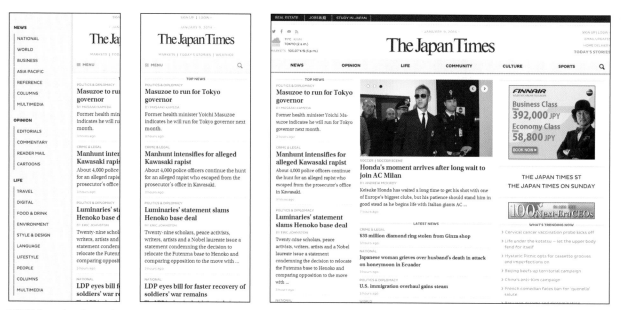

FIGURE 4: www.japantimes.co.jp

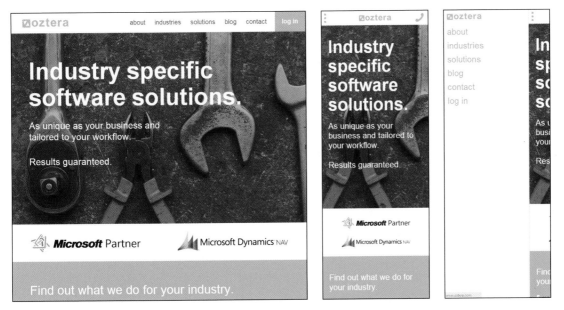

www.oztera.com

www.whisperism.com

08/Responsive Select Menus

One of the first solutions to responsive navigation was the use of select menus. In this model, a normal band of navigation options folds into a drop-down select control. Frankly, this approach has mostly fallen out of popularity. That said, I did happen upon a couple of examples that sort of used the approach. I say "sort of" because they put their own twist on it—they don't exactly have an actual HTML drop down control.

Despite an extremely small sample set, I opted to include this chapter because it inspired me. I was reminded of an approach that is no longer popular. In many cases, it was a terrible solution and I much prefer other approaches we use now. That said, I think it is always good to keep in mind the full range of options available to us so that we can always pick the best one. You might seldom use this approach, but that doesn't make it a bad option to keep on tap.

The Hudson's Bay Company (HBC) site **(FIGURE 1)** demonstrates a rather unusual problem. The navigation for this site is a single dropdown with an extensive list of links. This isn't your typical five-page site; it contains dozens of pages. Sure it isn't the biggest site, but the navigation they set up makes it an interesting site to work with. On the mobile version this remains a drop-down, but it has more of a select control feel to it. Again, it isn't what I would expect, but the results work well as I browse the site. The simplicity of packing all the menu items into a single drop-down is compelling.

The other example here, the Louis XIV site **(FIGURE 2)** demonstrates a more typical usage of the approach. Here a simple list of eight links is displayed as a single row of items on desktop and tablet computers. When it shifts to mobile, this row of links turns into a drop-down selection menu.

This approach in general stands in stark contrast to the frequent usage of navicons and menus that slide out from the side. I think the community has really settled in on these two options. I can't help but wonder what else we will come up with. The field is still wide open in my opinion, and we have yet to fully explore the possibilities.

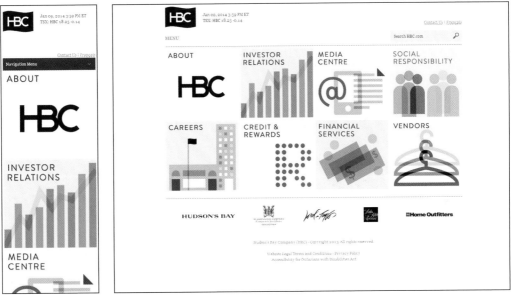

FIGURE 1: www3.hbc.com

FIGURE 2: www.louisxivenergy.com

08/Responsive Checkouts

There is no question: responsive design makes things far more complex to design and build. We have already seen how complicated it can get just figuring out how to show images in changing layouts. As I sort through the contents for this chapter on responsive checkouts, I suddenly feel like images are the least of our worries. E-commerce systems are extremely complex and involve so many situations and events. Transforming these interfaces into responsive things of beauty is a daunting challenge.

An intrinsic difference I keep coming back to is how users on desktops rely on clicks while mobile users rely on touches. This fundamental shift in interface methods is a significant to consider. It's also important to realize that the desktop version might be used in a more focused way at a desktop computer. In contrast, the mobile version might get used while someone is on the go and not giving it their full attention. Creating a single interface that accommodates all of this and optimizes the number of people completing the checkout is a considerable challenge. Frankly, it is no wonder that the community as a whole is really focused on a minimalist and simple style.

One thing that stands out to me with these samples is the "proceed to checkout" buttons. Not surprisingly, these buttons are styled to catch your attention. Most of them leap off the page and are impossible to miss. But something else stands out to me even more. I notice that on the mobile versions, many of the sites work hard to ensure that this key button is near the top of the page. This ensures that the button is visible on the default view from a mobile device.

Suitsupply **(FIGURE 1)** is a lovely example of this. As with many sites, the checkout button is both above and below the list of cart contents. And notice that the button remains very near the top of the page, helping to draw people into the process.

Another thing to observe is how the interfaces feel simpler, the smaller the screen gets. In most cases elements are just being moved down and end up off screen. The result is that the interface feels simpler and more focused. I can't help but wonder if a narrowed focus and reduction of clutter would benefit every screen size.

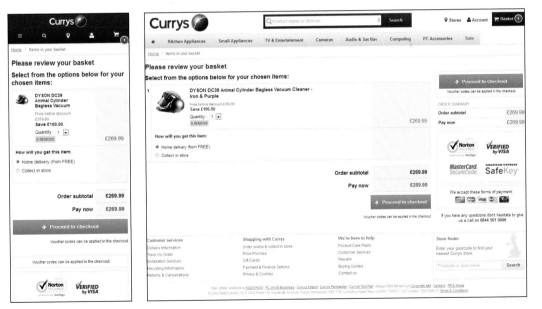

FIGURE 1: https://us.suitsupply.com/on/demandware.store/Sites-US-Site/en_US/Cart-Show

www.currys.co.uk/gbuk/o/initorder/basket-confirmation.html

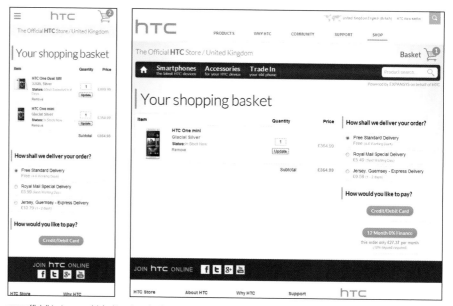

www.motelrocks.com/cart.php

www.officialhtcstore.com/uk/p_htc_store_basket.aspx

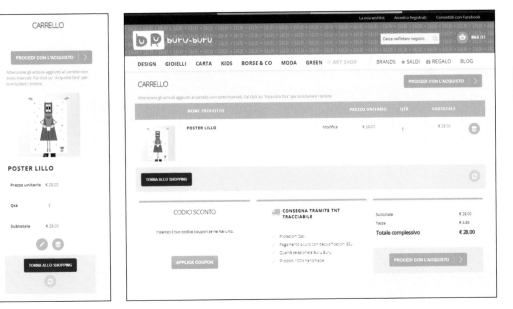

http://kershaw.kaiusaltd.com/cart

www.buru-buru.com/checkout/cart

08/Responsive Logins

Login forms are not nearly as complex as checkout systems, and therefore lend themselves to more exploration. I believe this is evident in the samples provided here. The most obvious approach is to essentially keep things the same, just shrink it down. This is exactly what the Whil website **(FIGURE 1)** does. The form is center-aligned and simply shrinks to fit the width of the screen. And guess what? It works really well. Sometimes the simplest approach is the best one.

The Salesforce login **(FIGURE 2)** page really caught my attention. The desktop version contains the normal login stuff, but it also includes links to some useful resources that help you maximize the system. I would propose that these resources are ideal for the desktop user exploring the application. In contrast, the mobile version hides these elements and just shows the login form (which, interestingly, didn't have to be reformatted or resized at all). On the mobile version, I suspect users are more interested in *using* the app and not in *learning to use* it. As such, the lack of distractions is reasonable and desirable.

Another example that got me thinking was the Campfire login **(FIGURE 3)**. On the mobile version, they opted to leave the logo out. On first take, this is almost shocking to think about. How could they not have their awesome little logo in there? And yet, it isn't there, and it actually works really well without it. I really appreciate their willingness to do something outside of convention for the sake of usability.

There are countless approaches to logins—which is kind of surprising considering what simple forms they are. The Starbucks site **(FIGURE 4)** presents another interesting concept. Here the desktop version has action buttons spread over two columns. It also includes a list of reasons to register an account. In contrast, the mobile version condenses the form into a neat little stack of action buttons and hides the benefits of joining. I can't help but assume that mobile users are more easily distracted and therefore it is logical to keep the path clear of shiny objects that might stop them. It also makes sense that someone selecting to visit the login page is already a customer, and therefore doesn't need to be sold on the product at all.

For me, the lesson I learn here is simple. Login forms (or any other fundamental part of a website) might be easy to ignore. But at the end of the day, our users can benefit greatly from some carefully thought-out design work. In fact, testing these interfaces with real users will likely provide extremely helpful insights.

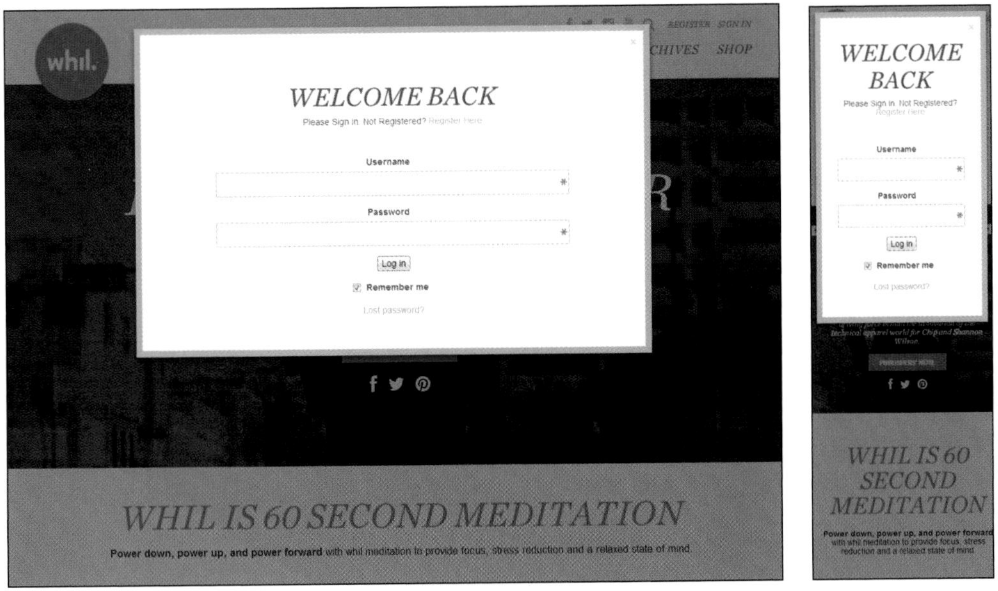

FIGURE 1: http://whil.com

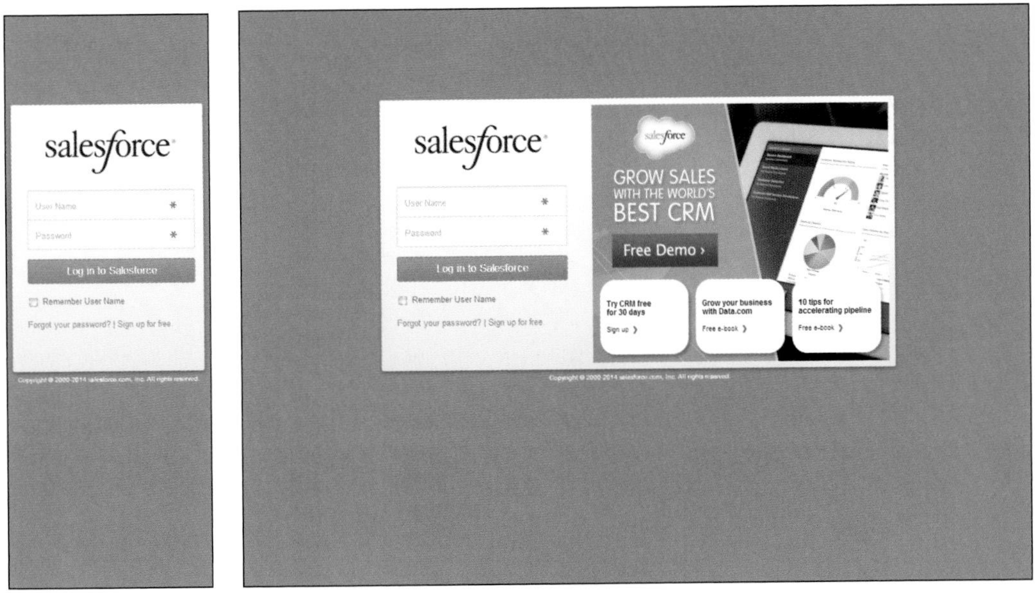

FIGURE 2: https://login.salesforce.com

FIGURE 3: https://launchpad.37signals.com/campfire/signin

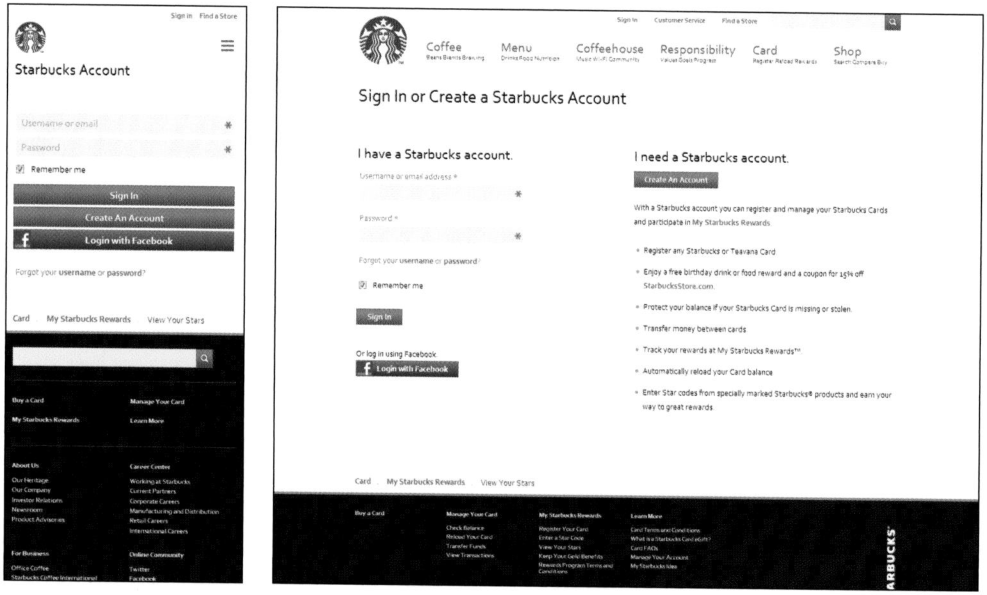

FIGURE 4: www.starbucks.com/account/signin

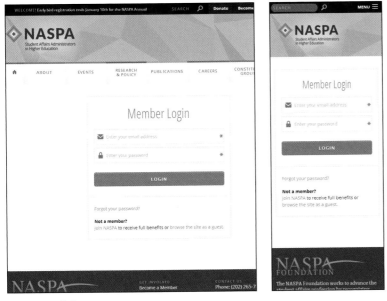

www.naspa.org/login

https://vllg.com/login

08/Responsive Priorities

Designers are slowly giving more attention to how needs change at different screen sizes. A user on a mobile site may have different reasons for visiting the site than a user on a desktop computer. The best example that comes to mind is someone visiting a restaurant's website. The desktop user might be exploring the idea of going there. They will need a wide range of information, such as location, menu items, photos to determine ambience, etc. In contrast, a mobile user might have sought out the destination's website to find what hours it is open, or to get directions. In other words, I suspect that many desktop users require more of a sales pitch, while mobile users just need the facts, as they are already interested in coming and may be on their way. Obviously, this is speculation, but it is easy to imagine. To fully understand users, it helps to observe them using your site.

One site that seems to embody the notion of responsive priorities is Jim 'n Nick's Bar-B-Q **(FIGURE 1)**. Contrast the mobile and desktop versions and I believe you will notice the difference rather quickly. The mobile version is a super-condensed set of buttons void of much distraction. I get the sense that they changed the priorities of the site as it adapted to different screen sizes.

Another example that vividly demonstrates this idea is the Kiwibank website **(FIGURE 2)**. The mobile version features three key action items front and center. These are very much focused on the tasks mobile users would be interested in doing. Contrast this with the more marketing-oriented desktop version of the site. It is clear that each version has a different priority and purpose for users, so adapting only makes sense.

The Garmin site **(FIGURE 3)** has its own interesting take on this concept. The desktop version features your typical marketing-type content. The mobile version, though it is there to sell the product, has a different approach to the same goal. The mobile site is first interested in the context users plan to use the product. I am intrigued that the mobile version takes this approach, but the desktop site does not.

An intimate understanding of your users and their goals will always be of use. The samples here remind us that those goals can (and likely will) change as the user changes modes. An on-the-go mobile phone user is almost guaranteed to have different goals then a desktop user stuck at the office.

FIGURE 1: www.jimnnicks.com

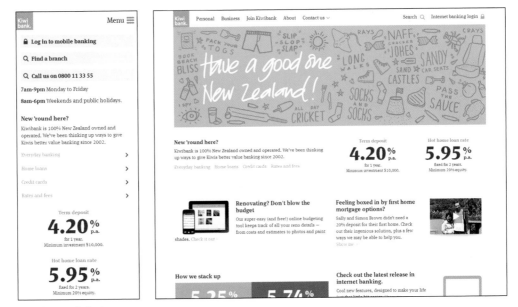

FIGURE 2: www.kiwibank.co.nz

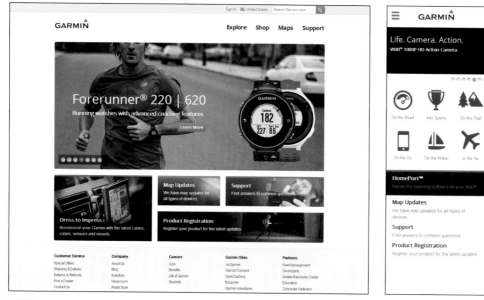

FIGURE 3: www.garmin.com

http://outpostdallas.com

http://cir.ca

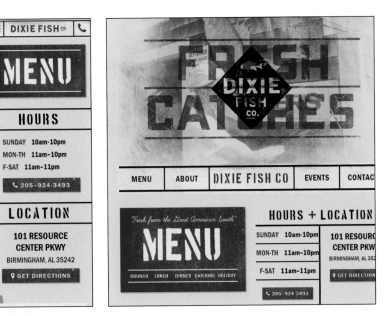

www.dixiefish.com

http://2013.ampersandconf.com

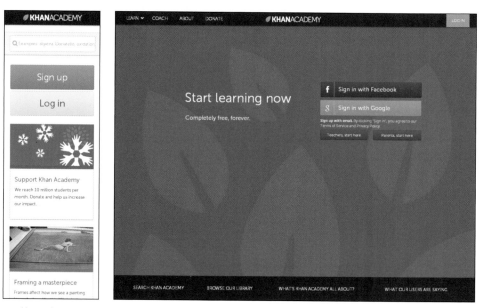

www.khanacademy.org

08/Responsive Bands of Content

I want to consider the structural strategies designers are using to create responsive sites. The first approach that the community gravitated toward was to create bands of content stacked on top of each other. Inside of these bands, the content would typically shift from multiple columns to a single stack of items. These bands of content would remain in the same stacking order across all screen sizes. In essence, this means that each band is operating independently of the others. Naturally, this makes designing, developing and maintaining sites like this much easier. Look at a few responsive sites and you will quickly spot this pattern, as it is tremendously popular.

The Stowe, Vermont website **(FIGURE 1)** is visually rich, and in this case, the bands of content don't feel overly simplistic at all. It feels natural and works really well. As the site condenses, each of the bands of content (I count five) simply adapts to fit the space available to it. There is no interaction between the bands of content; each functions on its own. The modular approach works well and it seems to me that maintenance on such a creation should be reasonable.

The pattern is pretty obvious once you notice. Consider the Hiut Denim Co. website **(FIGURE 2)**. Here the bands of content are even more obvious, as they are separated by heavy lines. Notice that the content never crosses these boundaries and again, each operates on its own. This stacked approach presents an interesting opportunity to vividly prioritize your content. If you consciously decide the order of things, important things will naturally rise to the top.

In some cases the structure is not obvious at first because the content and design of the site stand out so vividly. The Marco Grill site **(FIGURE 3)** demonstrates this. I immediately loved the site, but it took me a long while to realize that it used this pattern. I was captivated by the contents and not the layout.

Bands of content is what I would call a go-to style. It works remarkably well and ports nicely to code. What really gets interesting is how each of these individual bands are styled. They can be as visually rich and diverse as you want. Also, with the modular nature of the designs, I could easily imagine building a library of fundamental structures that can be reused and re-skinned for different purposes.

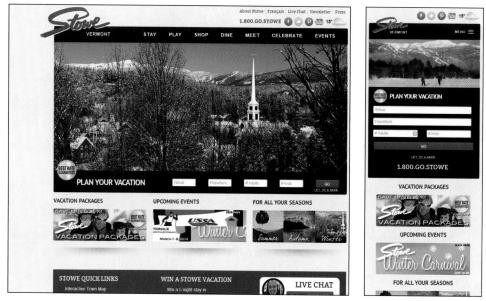

FIGURE 1: www.gostowe.com

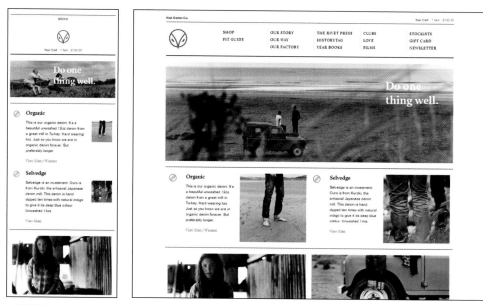

FIGURE 2: http://hiutdenim.co.uk

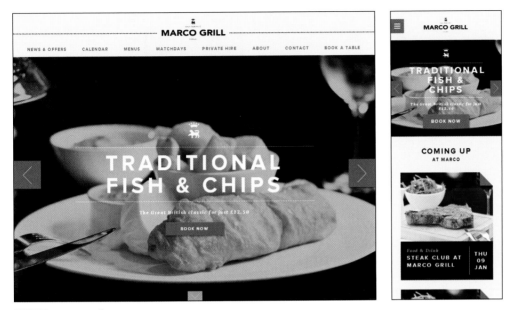

FIGURE 3: www.marcogrill.com

http://82birds.com

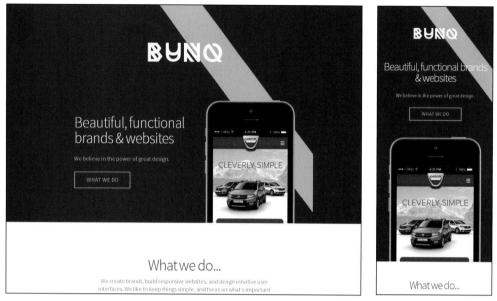

http://bunq.co.uk

http://hlynnphoto.com

08/Responsive Reformatting Layouts

I want to highlight responsive sites that change as the screen shrinks. But these sites do more than simply stack bands of content. In this case, the layouts are more complex, with the content interrelating in more complex ways. As the designs shift to mobile, there are more radical adjustments to the content. For me, this suggests a reprioritization of the content to suit each set of users. This very much relates to the responsive priorities chapter (page 248), but in this case, the layouts are all changing radically in fundamental ways. At times the two sites hardly even look like they go together.

A nice place to start is The University of Vermont website **(FIGURE 1)**. Here the two versions clearly represent the same organization, but the structures are radically different. Regardless of size, the page serves as a launching point to countless other pages and subsites. Notice the various ways the content was rearranged and re-factored to fit the smaller screen. These are not simple bands of content shrinking down.

The Advising Center of The University of Hawaii at Hilo **(FIGURE 2)** is another university site that also happens to demonstrate this idea. Not only does the focus of the site change, but the overall structure shifts to accommodate it. This one is really close to being bands of content, but for me there is a vivid change that goes beyond just packing things into smaller and smaller spaces.

The Oxo Tower Wharf website **(FIGURE 3)** is a rather unusual website to begin with. As it adapts to mobile, it undergoes some fairly radical changes. It's kind of funny, the more you look at it, the less radical it feels: I think the reality is that so much of the web right now is focused on a banded content approach that a more complex reformatting of the page feels so much more radical. I suspect that in time, layouts like this one will feel simple compared to what we will create. I believe the needs of mobile and desktop users are so far apart that soon reformatting layouts will be more common and extravagant.

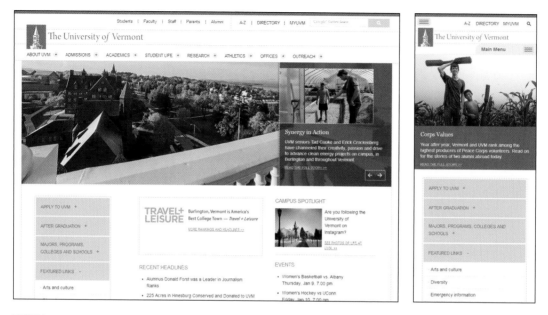

FIGURE 1: www.uvm.edu

FIGURE 2: http://hilo.hawaii.edu/~advising

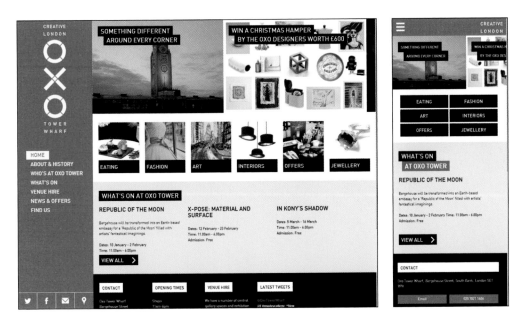

FIGURE 3: www.oxotower.co.uk

http://zioneceramica.es

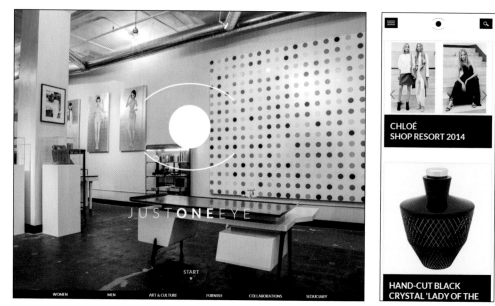

http://justoneeye.com

http://muumilaakso.tampere.fi

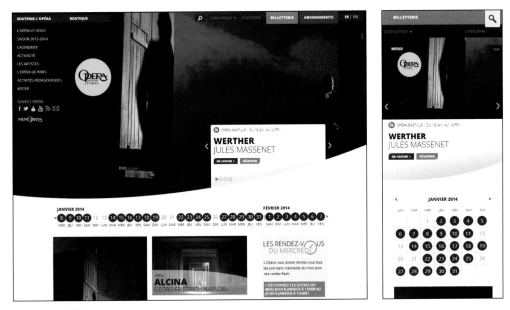

www.operadeparis.fr

http://adrianstourdefrance.com/event/tdf

INDEX

266

More Great Titles from HOW Books

The Mobile Web Designer's Idea Book
| Patrick McNeil

The Mobile Web Designer's Idea Book takes a close look at trends, styles, themes and patterns in mobile web design. You'll find the inspiration you need for your web design project as well as advice for analyzing trends and patterns that you can use to achieve the best mobile websites around. You'll find over 550 web design examples of the best mobile ebsites on the web today, along with commentary about what makes each of them great.

Above the Fold, Revised Edition
| Brian Miller

Above the Fold, Revised Edition breaks down the timeless fundamentals of effective communication within the context of web design, and presents them in an easy-to-understand format. Setting itself apart from other books on technology trends or timely design, this edition explores the essential aspects of good web design that won't go out of style, in order to effectively explain the thought process web designers go through when developing a successful web site.

For more news, tips and articles, follow us at **Twitter.com/HOWbrand**

For behind-the-scenes information and special offers, become a fan at **Facebook. com/HOWmagazine**

For visual inspiration, follow us at **Pinterest.com/HOWbrand**

Find these books and many others at MyDesignShop.com or your local bookstore.